WW2 SE20 & Me

Contents

Left: Juggler of five ration books and creator of miracle meals, she called "Winnie's Wangles", one of the real heroines of WW2 — my wonderful mum. Winifred Goldsmith, to whom this book is dedicated.

A quartet of Goldsmiths in 1944 (left to right) Dad – Bill Goldsmith, Uncles Dan and Jim, my brother Tony.

CHAPTER 1 - FARTING NOISES AND DEAD CATS

The sad-sounding man on the radio had said something about not receiving an undertaking from the German ambassador regarding a country called Poland and that, as a result, we were at war with Germany. Even to an eight-year-old lad like me, those words on the morning of Sunday, September 3, 1939, were no surprise - neither was the air raid warning which followed almost immediately. It sent all five of us - Mum, Dad, Tony, Margaret and me - scurrying downstairs from the top flat at 19 Thicket Road and several doors along to the basement flat of Mrs Shipstone and her two children, Dennis and Beryl, at number 13a.

Tony had the job of bringing the family's gas masks, each in its brown cardboard box and due to be carried, lugged, kicked or dropped in a variety of containers by each of us for the next five-plus years. The masks were another reason why the declaration of war was no surprise. They had been delivered one morning several weeks earlier. Like countless other youngsters, Tony and I had found that once the transparent eyepiece became fogged over, the only novelty of actually wearing this vital protection was to blow heavily and make it produce farting noises.

Now for a brief summary of who and where. At that time, Bill Goldsmith, head of the family, busy local journalist, was 35 years of age, and fluent in German as a result of many holidays in and around Frankfurt; my mother, Win, was two years older than Dad and had no occupation other than the considerable task of looking after Tony, 12, Margaret, just turned two, and me. We lived in Anerley, with a London postcode of SE20, and occupied a flat on the third floor of a house from which we had, to the south, extensive views across Beckenham and Elmers End towards and beyond West Wickham. This would eventually prove significant, as would the view to our right where we could see - beyond the nearby houses - planes using Croydon Airport.

The Shipstones had been friends of the family ever since we moved to number 19 in 1935, just after I started the autumn term at Anerley Infants' School. Mrs Shipstone used to describe herself as a "grass widow" because her husband was permanently absent. He had a veterinary practice in Penge and maintained his family reasonably well. Dennis was about five months older than I; Beryl - known for a long time as "Babe" - was five years old on the day we all sat around and waited for whatever that first air raid warning would bring. Then we heard the constant, unwavering note of what everyone would come to call "the All Clear" although leaflets from the authorities about Air Raid Precautions insisted that the signal was "Raiders Passed." If any raiders had passed, we certainly didn't hear them and so we picked up the brown cardboard boxes containing our gas masks and went back to the upstairs flat.

To say that war had "broken out" was an over-statement. There was nothing sudden about its arrival; even I knew about this apparently excitable man called Adolf Hitler who used to shut people into concentration camps. When Dennis and I had caught some grasshoppers and wanted to keep them in jars, Mrs Shipstone called us "little Hitlers" and shamed us into setting them free in the garden. During our family holiday at Folkestone in early August of 1939, we had seen trainloads of troops heading for the Continent; the BBC would soon be broadcasting "Garrison Theatre", an army-flavoured variety programme which featured a warm-voiced newcomer named Jack Warner who read comic letters from "my bruvver in the Life Guards". Among the catchphrases in the programme was the warning "Mind my bike!" which, like so many other phrases from wartime radio comedies, would become common linguistic currency guaranteed to raise smiles among people who were otherwise complete strangers to each other.

During the last of the motorcycle rodeos at the Crystal Palace stadium, on May 13th 1940, the commentator on the public address system trotted out the words "Mind My Bike!" when a couple of machines collided during one of the highly competitive events - and, of course, it raised an enormous laugh from the crowd. The sort of high jinks featured on these days usually involved flimsy chariots or prams pulled by motorcycles with dressed-up mechanics as passengers. But on this occasion there was also a javelin contest for which the targets were figures representing Hitler and one other, either Herman Goering or the Italian leader Benito Mussolini.

The figures came into the arena on the back of a lorry and the first was unloaded, then leaned against a backboard. Ready to launch their javelins were motorbike mechanics dressed as Romans and riding as passengers on machines that had already provided plenty of entertainment in various events earlier in the day. The new competition had a fairly simple format: each motorcyclist and his javelin-throwing partner would approach the target at a moderate speed; at a certain point the passenger would stand up and launch his missile at the target before the motorbike swerved away and returned to the rest of the dozen- or- so taking part. It was obviously a tricky routine, but the standard of marksmanship proved surprisingly good and the first target - Goering or Mussolini - received many hits.

With their aim improving, the gladiators retrieved the javelins and prepared to do even better with the brown-uniformed Hitler figure which was lifted down from the lorry and placed in position. The first motorcycle drove towards the target, the passenger raised his javelin - and the Hitler figure sprang to life and fled. As a collective gasp went up from the crowd, all the motorcyclists joined in the chase, caught up with the fugitive, surrounded him and then closed in as the javelins jabbed and probed. In less than a minute, and at some unseen signal, the melee was over, machines and men turned away leaving...an empty space. There was no sign of what had been the running target. “That man” had been wiped away by a clever piece of staging while surrounded by several thousand people. Thinking about it years later, the strange way in which the hunt concluded appears to have foreshadowed the eventual end nearly six years later of the man himself - surrounded by enemies as the world looked on, but leaving virtually no remains.

It now seems even stranger that people were enjoying a motorcycle rodeo and a speedway meeting on May 13th 1940. At that time the war on the other side of the English Channel and even further afield was turning into a disaster for the Allies. Before the end of May, we would be starting to evacuate troops from the beaches of Dunkirk. True, the printed programme for the speedway did carry a note that "in the event of an air raid warning, all visitors living within five minutes walk are advised to go home". For those who wanted to remain in the Crystal Palace grounds, it added that air raid shelters were provided "under the centre steps."

But let's return to the events of 1939. We all slept safely in our beds on the night of September 3, got up in the morning and, like Tony, I went to school. Turning from Thicket Road into busy Anerley Road, I saw a dead cat in the road and came across another further down towards the school. These were among the first victims of the nationwide blackout which had come into force and would cost the lives of people, as well as their pets, before we became used to having no street lights, while those who drove cars and buses peered through their windscreens and made whatever use they could of the light from heavily shaded headlamps. The road accident rate soared, and pedestrians suffered bumps, trips, and stumbles from lamp posts, trees, kerbstones, and gateways.

There was a huge demand for small electric torches, which triggered an immediate shortage of the size No. 8 batteries that most of them used. We were told - officially - that the flare of a match used for lighting a cigarette could be seen from several thousand feet in the air. Obviously those Luftwaffe pilots had very good eyesight, but we had not seen or heard anything of the German air force. Nevertheless, extra precautions had to be taken. At home, the routine in the evening was to put up the blackout at windows of any room in which there was a light. If you did not have heavy curtains, special lightproof black paper could be bought; later on, opaque black cloth became available. Resourceful handymen used it in frames which fitted over the windows at night; others fixed it around the windows with drawing pins. Air raid wardens patrolled the streets and householders who broke the blackout law could be fined. All theatres and cinemas were closed "until further notice" - but not for very long - and we were not to blow whistles, fly kites, or light bonfires at night. Somebody in the government must have taken to heart the early scenes of "Things To Come", the film based on H.G. Wells' book, in which the mythical and brightly lit Everytown is bombed from a sky filled with enemy aircraft, and people are crushed by the falling masonry of department stores and picture houses.

Reality for us was life being almost as usual. So far, only one thing was rationed - petrol - and we didn't have a car anyway. To jump a little way ahead and confound those who tell how "everything was rationed straight away", these are the dates on which commodities became available only through coupons: January 8, 1940 - bacon, butter and sugar; March 11, 1940 - all meat; July, 1940 - tea and margarine; March, 1941 - jam; May, 1941 - cheese; June 1, 1941 - clothes; July, 1941 - coal; January, 1942 - rice and dried fruit; February, 1942 - soap, tinned tomatoes and peas; July, 1942 - sweets (two ounces a week); August, 1942 - biscuits; and during 1943 - sausages.

The newspapers in those first days of the war had stories about pupils of London schools being evacuated but there was no mention of that for kids like us who lived, after all, in Kent - the northernmost reaches, admittedly, but in Kent. We felt smugly safe, and any passing car which carried a lot of luggage and looked as though its occupants were outward bound would receive shouts of "windy!" So it came as a shock when Mum and Dad announced that Tony and I would be going to live with my grandmother at 62 Bexhill Road in what everyone regarded as the south coast safety of Eastbourne.

We had not seen Gran since the previous year and she welcomed her two grandsons into an already busy home. She looked as formidable as ever and George Farrant, her long-time partner, still spent a lot of time on a chaiselongue to which clung the fruity smell of his Erinmore pipe tobacco. We lived and ate our meals in the large downstairs back room which led onto a scullery; the downstairs front room was still occupied by Bill Farrant, his wife Mona and their daughter Molly, who was about a year old. Bill, the only working member of the household, was still a turncock with the Eastbourne Water Company, came home every evening and washed himself in the scullery. This involved a kettle of boiling water which he poured into an enamel bowl in the sink. Bill had a habit of first putting the communal cake of Lifebuoy soap into the bowl and then pouring the water onto the soap, creating a froth and also making a hole in the piece of soap. He was always admonished by Gran - but never stopped doing it.

Hot water, incidentally, only came from kettles and saucepans heated on the gas stove in the scullery. The house had no bathroom but there was a tin bath hanging on a hook somewhere beyond the back door and, charged with a mixture of hot and cold, this took care of all-over cleanliness once a week whether, in the words of the old joke, we needed it or not. The loo was downstairs but not actually in the house, although it was under cover, also just beyond the back door. The house had three bedrooms, one of which Tony and I shared, and on the staircase leading to them was a narrow strip of carpet secured by brass stair rods which had to be taken out and polished every Saturday morning. Some of the lighter tasks in the weekly cleaning routine were allocated to us as new arrivals and the smell of Brasso and wax polish will always remind me of the well-ordered routine at Gran's house.

The next-door neighbour, Mrs Witham, who had two sons - Teddy and Brian - took on the job of finding us places at local schools. Tony, just approaching his 13th birthday, went mornings and afternoons to Bedewell School in Whitley Road, but the best that could be found for me was a place among the boys at St Andrew's in Seaside, already swamped with official evacuees from the Lambeth area. Sheer numbers meant being lumped in with the London kids and only attending the actual school building in the afternoons. What to do in the mornings with more than two dozen boys aged between eight and eleven years became a problem. At first the weather in late September and early October allowed us to spend a lot of time outside, in parks or on the beach, where a long-suffering and elderly master named Bert Moore did his best to keep us in order.

Mr. Moore had a hearing appliance with lots of wires and a hefty-looking battery which I at first took to be some sort of radio. As a security-conscious youngster who took to heart everything circulated by the Ministry of Information, I wondered whether Mr. Moore could be a German spy but then realised that the nation's enemies would hardly be interested in knowing that umpteen scruffy youngsters were playing football at Elm Grove, Hampden Park, and planned to write English essays at school in the afternoon. Looking back, I am amazed that we all trooped across the Lottbridge Drove - at the time a single track linking the east end of Eastbourne with Hampden Park - kicked a ball around in Elm Grove and made our way back again before going home to lunch (we called it "dinner") and then attending classes at St

Andrew's. Crossing the Drove also involved the occasional meeting with herds of cows, a novelty which tested the nerve of kids who were street-wise in London but not happy about getting close to huge creatures with horns. "If you're wearing anything with red in it, cover it up," said some of the more knowledgeable.

On another morning we were marched like troops down Seaside towards The Lodge hotel with Mr Moore at our head. Knowing that he had switched off his deaf aid to conserve the battery, the boys burst into song, using (or misusing) the tune of The Battle Hymn of the Republic about John Brown's body. The words were, "Old Bert Moore went"...(resounding raspberry)... "Against the wall. Old Bert Moore..." etc, three times, leading up to the fourth line, "And the wall came tumbling down!" Throw in a few choruses of "Glory, glory, hallelujah" and you get the picture, to which you can add the puzzled faces of passers-by who could not work out why an old gentleman, apparently in charge of a lustily abusive gang, took no notice of what they were singing. As the autumn weather took over, the Lodge Hotel - or a building next to it - became our morning rendezvous and we spent time in a small meeting room being told about the Bible, singing or taking part in games like Twenty Questions (long before it was on the radio). There was also a larger hall in which, on Friday mornings, we were joined by girls and someone who played the piano for country dancing. There was one called Brighton Camp and I can still remember the music for Flowers of Edinburgh although I never managed to get through the dance without making a mistake.

Back at Bexhill Road we seemed to have settled into a comfortable domestic routine, and I did not miss my parents very much. Each week they sent Tony and me a sixpenny postal order each, and we had to sit down on Monday evenings and write a letter home. Tony appeared to have no great problem with this, but for some reason I struggled with things to relate. We started by having to fill at least one side of a sheet of paper about the size of a page in an exercise book, but Gran allowed me to cut this down to half a page for a couple of weeks before a rebuke from Mum and Dad sent it back to a complete page again. If there was a budding journalist inside my head, he was hiding. What I missed most in the evenings was listening to the radio. It seems incredible now, but there was no radio in the house, and we relied only on newspapers and magazines. George Farrant would send me down to the newsagent's shop on the corner of Channel View Road and Seaside to get his evening paper, The Star. There was also the "Eastbourne Gazette" on Wednesdays and "Eastbourne Herald" on Saturdays, while the magazine intake included "War Illustrated" and, occasionally, "War News."

There were soldiers of the Royal Artillery in Eastbourne and I remember watching a drill parade on ground behind what was then the lifeboat house, with an officer ranting at one particular individual who had not, as far as I could see, done anything wrong. It struck me that being in the army was not very pleasant. The war itself was still something happening a long way off on the other side of the Channel. The magazines which appeared each week contained lots of morale-boosting pictures as well as articles about our servicemen and seemed to treat the whole thing as a continuation, following an interval of about 20 years, of the Great War. One of the regular features appeared under the heading “I Was There” with the title superimposed on a background of barbed wire. It recalled incidents and battles of the 1914 - 1918 conflict, and the inference was that Britain and its allies would win again. I still missed the radio, however, not so much for the news but for the increasing number of light entertainment programmes, many of them containing new catchphrases which classmates quoted.

Tony and I did, however, keep up to date with the film world. The Gaiety, nearby in Seaside, was one of our favourite cinemas, and we also went to one in Trinity Place which we called the News Cinema but later became part of the Classic chain. I can recall bits of the films we saw - mostly adventures - but only one title sticks in my mind. That was “Submarine Patrol” with a very young Richard Greene (he was later Robin Hood in the TV series) featuring the exploits of the United States Navy’s fast-moving surface vessels, known as subchasers, in the First World War. The film, as a recent check showed, was made in 1938, and even though we saw it in 1939, it would be another couple of years before America joined the more recent conflict.

"Conflict", however, was something of an over-statement. This was the period of what later became known as "the phoney war", in which very little happened anywhere, let alone Eastbourne. One of George Farrant's war magazines carried an item illustrated with a map of a tiny section of Kent and headed, "We have already captured this much of Germany", and so it looked as though events might go on for some considerable time. However, things livened up at sea, and in another part of the world when in mid-December we followed events in the Battle of the River Plate. The pocket battleship Graf Spee, damaged by cruisers of the Royal Navy, sought temporary refuge in the neutral harbour of Montevideo before heading out towards the sea and being scuttled by its captain, who then committed suicide. A few days later, at 62 Bexhill Road, Aunt Mona made a sponge cake which - taken from the oven too early - sank in the middle. We christened it "Scuttle cake", decided that it was too good to waste, and for several days enjoyed slices which had normal sponge at one end and gradually took on a toffee-like consistency towards the thin wedge end.

A couple of evacuee brothers at my school decided that they had seen enough of Eastbourne and tried to walk back to Lambeth. Their surname was Everitt, they were intercepted somewhere on the A22, brought back and pictured in the local paper. "That's them!" I said when Ethel Weymark, who lived next door at number 64, showed me the article, with their photograph, in the "Eastbourne Gazette." The older of the brothers was, a short while later, chosen to play the role of a happy beggar in a playlet called "A Bowl of Mist" to be produced as part of the school's Christmas celebrations. Yes, Christmas was on the way and with the weather getting much colder - heralding what was to be the start of a really bad winter - my fellow evacuees and I were no longer spending our mornings on aimless rambles with Bert Moore. We headed for The Lodge and a couple of hours on Bible studies and parlour games (apart from Friday folk dancing) before sitting in a proper classroom at St Andrew's during the afternoons. My ninth birthday arrived and I received from Uncle Bill and Aunt Mona a new harmonica to replace an old falling-apart instrument on which I could already suck and blow my way through "Keep the Home Fires Burning" and "It's a Long Way to Tipperary".

One evening Tony and I emerged from the cinema to find that it was snowing and we set off down Seaside, back towards Bexhill Road, trying to scrape together enough of the early fall to make a snowball. A bad-tempered man barked, "Leave it alone! F*****g snow!" and Tony, taking the moral high ground, looked at the departing gent and said, "He should be had up for bad language." The words "had up" were common parlance for "prosecuted" because strong language of that nature was not normally heard on the streets of Eastbourne, even if it was snowing. The fall did not last for long, so there would be no white Christmas, but that did not matter because Mum and Dad, with Margaret - then two years and four months old - were due to spend a few festive days with us.

It would be the first time that Tony and I had seen them since September, and I was looking forward to their arrival on what would also be the day of our school Christmas party. The boy and girl evacuees (the girls we only saw for country dancing on Fridays; where were they the rest of the time?) spent most of the day down at The Lodge. I cannot remember if we had a meal, but there were games which included a strange one-on-one hockey tournament played with upside down walking sticks and a small cloth bundle which served as a ball. A single school chair was placed at each end of the pitch and the idea, following a hockey-type bully-off, was to get the improvised rag ball through the legs of your opponent's chair. One of the kids managed to whack the ball home straight from the bully-off; I was hopelessly outpaced by an older girl and lost. I had never seen this game before and have never come across it again, but it was fun.

The grand finale to the party was a film show featuring Cicely Courtneidge in a comedy which involved her winning a tennis tournament and singing a song with the words, "Things are looking up, no matter what they say; things are getting better, better, better every day." It was a jolly, jaunty little tune and I sang it to myself while hurrying back to Bexhill Road where I knew that Mum, Dad and Margaret would be waiting. As I went in by the back door, through the scullery and into the main living room I could hear another tune - "Gee ain't it nice as we glide down the ice...whoops we go again". Mum, Dad and

Margaret were there - and Dad had brought the radio along as well.

CHAPTER 2 - WASHED OUT IN FRANCE

It was to be the first of six wartime Christmases, and I can only remember a few incidents within the overall pleasure of seeing my parents and young sister again. Among the presents was a boxed game with a twist on the old party favourite of "pin the tail on the donkey." It included a map of countryside across which ran a broad zig-zag stripe which represented the Siegfried Line. Also in the box were stiff paper cut-outs in the shape of socks, vests and shirts, together with several drawing pins. The game was called "Hang Out the Washing on the Siegfried Line" - after a topical song - and the idea was that, with the map secured against a wall or door, blindfolded competitors would take turns at trying to pin the items of washing on the zig-zag line. I don't think we ever played this game but - as with many boxed games - the bits and pieces hung around for weeks afterwards.

I would later, much later, come to know Michael Carr, the man - an American - who wrote the tune of "Hang Out the Washing on the Siegfried Line" (he also wrote "South of the Border" and many other well-known pieces) which in 1939 was one of those morale-boosting songs with words which within months would seem pathetic. For the benefit of the younger generation, this is how they went:

"We're going to hang out the washing on the Siegfried Line; have you any dirty washing, mother dear?

We're going to hang out the washing on the Siegfried Line for the washing day is here. Whether the weather may be wet or fine, we'll just rub along without a care. We're going to hang out the washing on the Siegfried Line - if the Siegfried Line's still there."

The line, named after the legendary hero, was Germany's well-fortified defence along its western border but we - the Allies - had our own French-built Maginot Line, although it petered out when it reached Belgium. Our great military minds were still stuck in the muddy trenches of 1914-18.

There was another song in 1939 - "Run, Rabbit, Run" - which I had only heard other children singing until Mr and Mrs Witham of number 60 Bexhill Road invited Gran, Tony, and me next door to a Christmas party with their sons, Teddy and Brian. They not only had a combined radio and record player but they had a record of Flanagan and Allen singing "Run, Rabbit, Run", which they played at full blast during a sing-song that preceded tea and games. I knew most of the words and can still remember my grandmother smiling at me as I joined in. Sadly, that is the last memory I have of her smiling, because events were soon to take a downturn.

With Christmas over, Mum and Dad, with Margaret, returned to Anerley, but within a few days my grandmother's health began to decline. She had difficulty climbing the stairs to the front bedroom and tried spending the night on the downstairs sofa but was found in the morning sitting on the floor with the bedclothes draped around her. To Aunt Mona, who was gradually taking overall charge of the home, she dictated a letter asking my mother to come and see her as soon as possible. As it was being written, Tony said, "Why don't you send it in an envelope with a black border?" He meant it as a joke but I didn't think it funny. Gran was taken back upstairs for what proved to be the last time.

Tony and I had resumed post-holiday school, the pre-Christmas snow had all gone but there was an uneasy feeling at 62 Bexhill Road. Aunts and uncles called in, my mother arrived on her own and conversations were kept at a level barely above a whisper. My grandmother died on Thursday, January 11, 1940, but nobody took me to one side to break the news. Tony may have been told but it must have been at least a day or two afterwards that I plucked up the courage to ask Aunt Mona, "Has granny died?" She blinked a few times and nodded without saying anything. I would have asked my mother but she had gone back home, and I had barely missed her amid all the comings and goings.

Two or three nights later George Farrant asked Tony and I to come and see Gran for the last time. He led us to the front bedroom where, on the old-fashioned brass bedstead, a figure lay completely covered by a white sheet. He pulled back the upper part of the sheet and there was Gran, white, quiet and cold. "Put your hand on her forehead and you won't dream about her," said George. I did so without hesitation but Tony said "Ooer!" before he was eventually persuaded. I cannot remember why, but George and Bill Farrant took me with them when they went on a walk along the seafront. This was before the funeral, so they either had things to discuss or may have even needed to keep me out of the house while arrangements were being made - perhaps the removal of Gran's body by the undertaker. The walk took us to the far end of the promenade, by the lifeboat museum, before we turned back and I, in wellington boots and wrapped up against the January weather, was allowed to crunch my way across the shingle to the sands exposed by the low tide. With waves on my right, I kept pace with George and Bill on the promenade while marching and singing "Onward, Christian Soldiers". When I eventually re-joined them I offered the thought, "At least Gran won't have to go through the war." Yes, it was still going on somewhere but would get a lot closer within a few months.

Tony and I did not attend Gran's funeral. We were looked after for most of the day by the people at 64 Bexhill Road and allowed to peep discreetly through the front room curtains when the hearse and other cars arrived next door. Later, after they had returned from Ocklynge Cemetery, I noticed that the Mum was wearing what had previously been her brilliantly coloured evening coat. Back at home in the summer I used to open her wardrobe and admire the golden glow of such a coat as I had never seen before. Now it was dyed black and would never be the same again. As if to catch the mood, that night the weather turned and produced one of the heaviest snowfalls in years. It was the first of several near-blizzards which kept Tony and me, now in the care of Mona and Bill, fully occupied in the business of keeping warm on our separate ways to and from school.

The snow eventually disappeared, but there was flood water in many places in our part of the town. In Princes Park, the lake crept well beyond the paved surround and up the paths which led from the area surrounded by a running track. Parts of the Crumbles, which backed onto houses in Seaside, had sheets of deep water which tempted some of the more daring evacuees to try boating. With the Lambeth kids I was still going down to The Lodge in the mornings, and at the point where we passed the entrance to the Lottbridge Drove, a disused single railway line crossed the main road and carried on across the Crumbles. There, on the right as we walked away from the town, was a large gap opening onto the expanse of flooded waste ground - and in the middle of it one morning was a tatty-looking rowing boat carrying three or four lads who were managing to propel the craft by using lumps of wood as paddles. They reached dry land and tumbled out while their school friends all cheered. Where they had managed to acquire the boat was a mystery - and it had disappeared by the time we headed back up the road after school.

The war moved a little closer on March 20, 1940, when the 5,439-ton cargo ship SS Barn Hill, en route from Canada, was bombed in the Channel off Eastbourne and caught fire. Most of the crew were rescued by the town's lifeboat, Jane Holland, and the ship, with the aid of tugs, was eventually beached near Langney Point.

A fuller account of the Barn Hill incident is well worth reading (The Blitz Then and Now, volume one). Tony found on the beach a coil of rope he reckoned had come from the Barn Hill, which we could see over to our left as we stood on the shingle near Channel View Road. We were not among the many people from the east end of Eastbourne who made their way to the sands near the wreck at low tide and helped themselves to much of its cargo, including tinned food from which the sea had removed the labels.

There was still no radio at 62, the last-but-one house in Bexhill Road, but Uncle Bill came home with a wind-up gramophone and selection of records which provided some extra amusement. We were still relying on George Farrant's evening newspaper, The Star, for news of the war, which contained names of far-off places. He would sometimes venture down to The Archery pub in the evening and, returning on one occasion, managed to enter through the back door of the last-but-one house in Latimer Road before realising his mistake. He blamed the blackout and the fact that there was no moon; the rest of us sniffed the alcohol-laden atmosphere and smiled at each other. In fairness, anyone who knows that area of identical houses and back alleys would understand his confusion.

With the weather improving, I settled into a comfortable routine of school and play. There were swings and slides at nearby Princes Park and each Wednesday lunchtime Aunt Mona made deliciously aromatic bacon pudding containing herbs. Then in March or April, I cannot remember exactly, Tony said that he and I would be going back to Anerley. We packed our few belongings, said goodbye to George Farrant, Uncle Bill, Aunt Mona and the increasingly pretty young Molly and caught the train from Eastbourne station. There to meet us at East Croydon were my mother and Dennis Shipstone. The following Monday I returned to Anerley Junior School and saw again many of the friends - and a few not-so-friendlies - I had left there just over six months previously.

With Tony, there was a difference. Instead of returning to the secondary school in Oakfield Road, Penge, he went to Beckenham Technical College - which has since made me wonder if that was one of the reasons we had returned from Eastbourne. To explain: the great educational divide at that time was the country-wide 11-plus (it still is in some parts) which no Goldsmith in our family has ever passed. Later, however, another opportunity was given for non-academics with a spark of practical ability by setting a series of tests which determined whether they could go to technical school. Tony, who had always been particularly good at drawing, started at Beckenham Tech, which involved a bus journey (until he acquired a bicycle) and - horror of horrors - classes on Saturday mornings.

In the meantime, school hours at Anerley were being changed. Somebody had worked out that having kids trooping to and from school twice a day actually doubled any risk of being caught in the open by enemy action. The new idea was that we started school at 8.30am and finished at 2.30pm. We took sandwiches and ate them with milk during a half-hour break - and, apart from having to get up earlier than usual, the kids approved of the new arrangement.

I was always in the A stream at junior school where there were also B classes of kids who mainly seemed to come from the rougher parts of the locality, like Ridsdale Road, St Hughes Road and Castledine Road. On my return from Eastbourne, the timid Miss Ellins who had tried to teach me in 1A seemed to have disappeared and in any case I was up into 2A where we had a Mr Macleod for most of the time and an eccentric lady, Miss Ling, for the rest. In what was to be an increasingly troubled 1940, classes and teachers were constantly swapped around. One of the men, a Mr Bullock who taught in the B stream, left to join the army and nobody was sorry because he was rather too active with the cane. Within a couple of weeks following his departure, boys in what had been his class were reporting that "Mr Bullock has been killed in action" - which turned out to be complete fiction.

Mr Macleod was, for most of us, our first male teacher, and his style was relaxed with a certain amount of humour. While this was at first a refreshing change, I came to realise that he got most of his laughs from the girls and that he had favourite targets among some of the less able boys. For a while I had a lad named Cyril Canning sitting next to me. He was obviously a borderline case who would have been happier in the B stream, but he was cheerful and he tried his best. Macleod picked on him because his clothes were scruffy and, when Cyril turned up in something a little more suitable, picked on him again because he had tried to improve his appearance. After that Cyril stopped trying and eventually, following an unexplained absence, was said to have been caught by the police stealing a bicycle. We never saw him again and, even at nine years old, I couldn't help wondering whether a little more kindness and a little less mockery might have made a difference.

When Tony was in Macleod's class a few years earlier there was a boy called Jimmy Walpole who could not pronounce words like "view" or "new"; they came out as "voo" or "noo." He was made to stand in front of the other pupils and recite "The Glory of the Garden" by Kipling, which opens with the lines, "Our England is a garden that is full of stately views, of borders, beds and shrubberies and lawns and avenues…" There were muffled giggles at the resulting mispronunciations; it was not a kind way to treat a lad. Jimmy's family, who lived in Anerley Road near the junction with Thicket Road, had created a bomb shelter in their basement flat, complete with a flag to be poked out of the wreckage in emergencies. It read, "Please help us. We are trapped." We thought it was hilarious - but this was early in 1940.

Dennis Shipstone was also in the class and we continued to be good friends, joined, at about this time, by Ian Robinson, who lived across the way from us at 8 Thicket Road. None of us had bicycles, so we didn't venture very far during out-of-school hours, and there was little traffic to bother us in our various street games in which we were occasionally joined by other children whose parents had rented nearby flats but never seemed as permanent as our own families. There were other friends who lived a little farther away but always formed part of the same group in the school playground. Among these were Len Quinnell, who had been around since infants' school, Pat Aylward, and David Kidson. When Dennis Shipstone and I managed to share a double desk in Mr Macleod's class, Len Quinnell was immediately behind us and provided the occasional distraction by quietly singing verses of "Mary From the Dairy" when our teacher was otherwise engaged. Dennis and I were intrigued by the name Quinnell and Len managed to keep a straight face while assuring us that he was of Russian origin.

In the wider world, things were happening. In early April, the Germans invaded Denmark and Norway, although British troops went - unsuccessfully - to Norway's rescue in mid-April. The newspapers, BBC radio news bulletins, and newsreels at the cinema assured everybody that there was no need to worry - and our side always told the truth, or so we believed. Being back at home after Eastbourne meant that we listened to the radio every day but - and this is important - the news was not broadcast until 7pm each evening. It was a prewar agreement between the newspaper proprietors and the

BBC which continued into 1940 but ceased when the pressure of events brought an end to what had been a cosy arrangement. (According to the BBC website, more frequent daily bulletins were introduced as soon as war was declared, but I have a memory of my father in 1940 pointing to the additional items, highlighted in the Radio Times, and commenting that it was about time the BBC came up to date.)

Throughout this time, possibly as a result of all those war magazines I had been reading, I was convinced that our forces were firmly entrenched in France and would eventually wear the Germans down. So it was disturbing when news broke in May that enemy troops had been landing by parachute in Belgium and Holland. Had I not read in one of Dad's aviation magazines that such a thing was impossible? Obviously the Germans had not seen the article by Brigadier Whoeveritwas (Retired). Among the songs on the radio was "My Sister and I", telling the story of a Dutch boy and girl fleeing from the invading enemy. The middle eight bars of it ran, "We're learning to forget the fear that came from a sudden sky. We're almost happy over here but sometimes we wake up at night and cry." It ended, "My sister and I recall once more the fishing schooners pulling into shore and the home that was all our own before...but we don't talk about that." We sang it at school and when the BBC was due to broadcast a programme about two children who underwent the horrors of invasion before escaping from Holland, we were told to listen.

The news was still full of place names - the sort of cities that we had only seen in an atlas at school or - and then they really used to have them - on the illuminated dials of radio sets. The names of important-sounding people were also cropping up, along with words like "national" and "government." Adults, particularly men, seemed preoccupied with the latest news whereas my friends and I were only interested in warmer weather and longer days as the month of May wore on. It was, of all things, the appearance of strange coins that finally woke me to the seriousness of the war situation.

Some of the children at school started showing each other coins of a type none of us had ever seen before. It was money with heads that were not George V, George VI or even Queen Victoria; there were words like "centime" and "franc" and - wonder of wonders - some of these coins had been minted with holes through the middle. It was obviously foreign - but why had so much of it appeared so suddenly? The penny - or centime, or franc - finally dropped one afternoon when some friends and I followed a column of soldiers marching up Anerley Road to the Crystal Palace Low Level station. How they actually came to be in Anerley Road did not concern me at the time, although many years later I learned that they had been billeted at the temporarily vacant School for the Deaf in Versailles Road. With an increasing number of other children, we followed them until they halted in the forecourt of the station, then filed down to one of the platforms. The last soldier to leave the forecourt was a sergeant who smiled as he turned to face the crowd of children pressing forward with their hands outstretched. With a final mischievous grin, the sergeant reached into his greatcoat pocket, produced a handful of foreign coins and tossed them to the children.

It was at that moment I realised the truth; those and all the other strange coins had come from soldiers who no longer needed them. We had been forced out of France.

To conclude this chapter on an unusual but still apposite note, I want to move back a few days in May 1940 and away from Anerley to somewhere near the French city of Lille and one small unit of British troops in the Royal Corps of Signals. For most of them, being in France was not only their first time abroad but also their first experience of being at war. They were lucky, however, in that their warrant officer was a veteran who had seen active service during the First World War. He had also sent a postcard to his wife and family, adding his special regards to a fictitious Lily - which somehow evaded the censor and conveyed his location to those at home.

The unit already knew that the so-called phoney war was over and the German army was on the move. For a day or two, heavy gunfire could be heard to the south - that was in the direction of the French-built and heavily fortified Maginot Line - as signal traffic increased. Then, on one vital morning, the warrant officer could hear a different pattern in the firing - it had switched to the east -

and he went to report this to the commanding officer. The CO was not to be found, and in fact was never seen again, so the warrant officer took command of the detachment.

From the new direction of the gunfire, it was obvious to him that the Germans had simply side-stepped the Maginot Line by crossing into Belgium and that, along with thousands of other British troops, his unit of signallers was in danger of being caught in an outflanking movement. In one respect, they were perhaps fortunate that Lille was so close to the Belgian border and that they - or at least the warrant officer, by drawing on previous experience - could tell what was happening. When communication with other units broke down it was time to go, and the signallers moved out. Their retreat was carried out in an orderly way and they stayed together, bound by the normal sense of comradeship to be found among troops who have worked closely with one another and also by their trust in the senior man who had become their leader.

It was his judgement, as a veteran soldier who had also served in India, that kept the unit intact by not always taking the obvious line of retreat. They arrived at Dunkirk, stayed together during the evacuation, and returned unscathed to a shocked but grateful England. Having succeeded in saving his unit, the warrant officer managed to get immediate leave and travel to Belfast where he knew that his wife, two sons, and daughter would be wondering what had happened to him. He arrived at the house in the early morning and the front door was opened by his younger son. The old soldier dipped into his greatcoat pocket and then dribbled a handful of sand into his son's outstretched palm. "There you are," he said. "That's all the way from the beach at Dunkirk." Reunited with his family, he went to bed and slept for two days.

The old soldier was Alfred Costello, who went on to become the longest serving senior warrant officer in the Royal Corps of Signals. The nine-year-old youngster who received the sand was the Alfred Costello who, 15 years later, would marry my sister Margaret.

CHAPTER 3 - MUM! THEY'RE DIVE-BOMBING!

If Britain stood alone - as indeed it did at this time in June 1940 - what was happening with the rest of the family? The only professional soldier was Uncle Dan, from whom we heard occasionally, tucked away in India and a long way from the Germans. The scruffy Uncle Jim was by this time in the army and - according to him - became involved the unsuccessful attempt to oppose the German occupation of Norway. He was still in uniform four years later and, as a picture of him with Dad, Dan and Tony shows, was still a private. Dad joined the ARP - later Civil Defence - as did Uncle Charlie in Eastbourne. The only other full-time soldier by that time was Uncle Tom, Rose's husband, for whom joining up was initially a short move from his home in Folkestone to the barracks at Shorncliffe, although he was afterwards transferred to Goole in West Yorkshire and later served overseas in the Mediterranean area, including Malta.

I don't think any of us ever met Aunt Maisie's other half. The phrases "other half" and "significant other" were not used in those days and she did eventually get married to Lionel Angel who was the father of Maisie's first child, Carol - and he also went into the army. Dad's youngest sister had stayed in the Shepherd's Bush area and was among the people who used to turn up occasionally on Sundays. There was also a notable pre-war Christmas when Maisie, among many seasonal visitors to our flat, spent a couple of days stretched out on a three-seater settee we had on the landing. She had gone to the pub with Dad's crowd, announced her intention of getting drunk, and succeeded.

I am not sure when Carol was born, but she was about a year younger than my sister Margaret and stayed with us for a week in 1940 when Maisie, effectively a single mother and needing to go to work, asked Mum if she could be a foster parent. Maisie left her with us and Carol spent two days crying at the doorway to our flat and refusing to eat. Eventually she began to settle and play with Margaret, then approaching her third birthday. Mum wrote to Maisie, telling her not to visit on the following Sunday because it would upset Carol all over again, but Maisie turned up and Mum told her to take Carol back. For all its good intentions, it had become an upsetting episode and I have to confess to turning away from the disturbing sight of Mum trying to force-feed a toddler who only wanted her real mother. Poor Carol; I last saw her in 1980 when Dad, Brandon, and I were on our way to the Continent and travelled by ferry from Ramsgate where Maisie, by then Mrs Gillespie, was living.

We called at her home in Ellington Road and Carol was there, looking dreadfully ill. She died shortly afterwards, in her early 40s.

Back to Anerley in 1940 and an early summer during which air raid sirens were still only heard occasionally. But there were signs of international events. Who, we wondered, were the strange men who gathered in the evening at Betts Park? They were not in uniform, they sat on the grass in a group of twenty or more and gabbled at each other in a tongue none of us could understand. They were not friendly or unfriendly; they were just there.

"Refugees - from Belgium," said an old lady we all knew as Half-hundred. She was a lively character who lived at 8 Thicket Road and the nick-name was a legacy of her 50th birthday, which she had celebrated with a very noisy party, announcing that she was halfway to being one hundred. Ever since, it was a case of "Look - there goes old Half-hundred" and, to be fair, she quite enjoyed the title.

There were some younger refugees as well, and a couple of boys started attending our school - even though they didn't understand English. One of them was taken to the school dentist in Oakfield Road where many of the lad's teeth were removed. For several days it seemed from his reaction that he would have preferred to stay with the Germans. Eventually he and the others all disappeared from the scene.

Another sign of things to come: a battery of anti -aircraft guns was installed in the open ground beyond our school wall - but we still had not seen any German aircraft. We acquired some new neighbours, the Hughes family, in the two upper floors of 10 Thicket Road, immediately opposite our place. Mr Hughes seemed to be something in the City and played a baby grand piano in front room; Mrs Hughes and their daughters, Joyce and Gwen, all spoke in a refined manner and were very friendly.

Tony's attendance at Beckenham Tech produced a chance for some of the boys to go fruit picking near Goudhurst in Kent, and they returned with all sorts of lurid stories about seeing aerial dog fights - Spitfires and

Hurricanes taking on German fighters and bombers. As proof, Tony had brought back pieces of what he said were shot-down aircraft. It was aluminium and had all the appearance of having suffered, but why had these raiders not ventured nearer to us in south east London? We did not have to wait much longer.

As already mentioned, our flat at the top of a four-storey house on the rising ground of Anerley had wonderful views across and beyond Beckenham, towards West Wickham and perhaps even farther during the clear, warm summer evenings of August. It was easy to relax by just sitting at the open windows of the lounge. Over to our right we could occasionally see numbers of aircraft approaching the old Croydon Airport, by then an RAF station, and watch them descend and eventually disappear behind the intervening houses. The evening patrol, we told ourselves, had come home.

On Thursday, August 15, the aircraft which approached Croydon in the early evening did not show any signs of landing; instead, they began circling. For my mother, Tony, and I watching from the lounge windows, this was an interesting variation, made even more entertaining when single planes began diving, pulling up and rejoining the whirling circus. A nagging suspicion made me look more carefully as yet another aircraft swooped; I saw it drop something small and black. "They're dive bombing!" I shouted. Tony and my mother told me not to be so stupid, so I told them to watch as the next plane pulled out of its dive.

Sure enough, another black dot detached itself.

Mum looked around wildly. "Where's Margaret?" she wanted to know. Margaret was probably with Beryl Shipstone, and by the time she had been found, the raid on Croydon Airport was all over. The aircraft were heading back south, and it was another twenty minutes before the air raid warning was sounded. We had at last seen the enemy in action. That night the sirens went again and, before I had a chance to get out of bed and get dressed, I heard bombs falling for the first time. A glimpse through the blackout curtains showed two fires blazing towards the south-east. We fled down two flights of stairs to the hall, down the front steps and then along the road to Shipstones in the basement of 13 Thicket Road. It was the first of many such dashes in the coming months.

With hindsight, it is now obvious that what Tony and his technical school friends had seen in Kent was part of the Luftwaffe campaign aimed at knocking out RAF fighter stations in preparation for a cross-Channel invasion, which required complete control of the air. It had yet to be called the Battle of Britain but that, from its first skirmishes in May to the final throw in mid-September, is what it was. August 15 had been designated Eagle Day by the Germans because they mounted a huge number of synchronised attacks against targets stretching from the north east of England to the south-west. According to Volume 1 of "The Blitz Then and Now" the group of aircraft we saw from our front windows had originally intended to attack the RAF airfield at Kenley but failed to find their target in the evening haze and moved on to Croydon instead.

That particular day in August marked a turning point because it resulted in Reichsmarschall Herman Goering, who commanded the Luftwaffe, realising that he was losing too many aircraft. The bombers we had seen were twin engine Messerschmitt 110s, of which six were shot down, plus one escorting ME 109 fighter. This contributed to a total of 151 enemy aircraft lost in a series of major actions - the greatest number on the Western Front in a single day throughout the whole war including (although that was to come) September 15. What had started as Eagle Day became known in the Luftwaffe as Black Thursday.

In Eastbourne, which London education authorities as well as my parents had considered to be safe, enemy activity against the town had begun on July 17. According to Aunt Rose (of whom more in a moment) there were daylight raids during which George Farrant stood in the backyard of 62 Bexhill Road peering through binoculars at aircraft and remarking loudly, “Swaddikas? I can’t see no blasted swaddikas!” If he was looking for *swastikas*, he would have needed stronger field glasses. The small crooked cross symbol only appeared on tailplanes but he should have been able to see the large black iron crosses painted on the wings and fuselage.

By this time, with Uncle Tom in the Army, Rose and young Geoff had moved from Folkestone back to

Eastbourne and were probably at Bexhill Road with her father George Farrant, half-brother Bill and his wife Mona, plus Molly. And as far as Tom was concerned, there was only one safe place for his wife and son - America. Tom's family were still there, probably in or near Detroit, and a number of ships carrying evacuees had already crossed the Atlantic safely.

I am most grateful to Geoff Woodward for having preserved two letters from his father - army number 6404219 - then in D Company of the Royal Sussex Regiment at Goole, West Yorkshire. Neither is dated, but it was obviously the summer of 1940, and both catch the mood of a soldier whose family, almost 300 miles away, is in danger.

The first, written on a Saturday afternoon, says: "I shall be very relieved when you are out of this country. You have seen more action than I have. You shouldn't have gone out into the street when they were machine gunning. Don't forget that bullets ricochet and whizz into any old corner where they are least expected. You really must remember to keep off the streets and when indoors to keep away from the windows and if possible to lay or sit on the floor. I had to send that telegram as the wireless at 0700 hrs this morning said that there had been a deliberate bombing raid on Eastbourne."

The second letter, written a few days later, confirms that plans for the trans-Atlantic evacuation of Rose and Geoff were already being made. Tom says: "I was most relieved to get your letter. In spite of your wire, I was still thinking all sorts of things; I expect I shall be until you are safely away in the States. What a dastardly thing to do; there is absolutely no object of importance at Hampden Park, surely? Just indiscriminate bombing of helpless civilians; no wonder the wireless made the most of it."

It continues, "I'm so glad that your passage is registered but I don't quite gather what you mean by not liking to write to Dad for the money draft. You must write and tell him at once what Pickfords say about him making over the money to them. Don't forget to wire me immediately you know the date, otherwise I shan't see you at all and I couldn't bear that. Now don't let foolish pride stop you from writing to Dad about the money. Just think of Geoff's face when the bombers come over."

Despite all this, Rose and Geoff remained in England and were evacuated to Wotton under Edge in Gloucestershire. In any case, sailing to America was no longer safe; on September 18, 1940 the City of Benares was torpedoed in the Atlantic and 83 of the 90 children on board were killed.

I have a memory of Rose and Geoff coming to 19 Thicket Road and staying at least one night during 1940. Whether this was at a time when Rose was in London, trying to fix up a passage to America, I cannot recall, but I do remember her telling us the story of George Farrant, the binoculars and the "blasted swaddikas." On a sadder note, and moving ahead in time for a few lines, I also remember hearing later in the war that Rose and Tom were expecting another child. By the time the baby, a girl, was born Tom was overseas and Rose had the child at a nursing home somewhere in the West Country. It was a live birth and Rose called the baby Angela but was later told that the baby had died before it could even be registered. Many years later she was still mystified by the tragedy and deeply suspicious of one particular doctor because around that time at the same home a number of other mothers in similar circumstances had also lost babies. It was one of those things which in a country at war tends to get pushed aside.

As the summer of 1940 wore on in Anerley we became used to the sound of air raid warnings and realised that the wardens - still with "ARP" on their steel helmets at this stage - were doing a useful job. Months earlier we had laughed at their dark blue uniforms, the yellow gas capes and the officious attitude that far too many of them displayed. One in Lullington Road, whose garden backed onto our's, was the typical little man with a big attitude. At about this time, Private Jack Warner of BBC radio's Garrison Theatre was, according to the script, promoted to lance corporal and started calling himself "one-stripe Warner." Coincidentally, our bumptious neighbour in the ARP acquired a stripe so we all called him "one-stripe warden." Not exactly in the Noel Coward school of sophisticated wit, but it amused us.

Back at school we were all herded down to the basement whenever the sirens went and nearly jumped out of our skins as the anti-aircraft battery a few hundred yards away started firing. Wellington at the Battle of Waterloo allegedly made a remark about the appearance of his troops - "I don't know what they do to the enemy, but they scare the shit out of me." Something like that. Had I, in my nine-year-old wisdom, known about that part of history, I would have agreed with him as far as the AA guns were concerned.

After the Luftwaffe's Eagle Day raids against RAF airfields had turned into Black Thursday, the German air force paid more attention to the civilian population of cities, especially London. The first bomb on the City itself fell on August 25. On that same night, the RAF started night raids on Germany, including one on Berlin which infuriated Hitler. When the Luftwaffe came over by day and were intercepted by RAF fighters as they approached London from the south we could, from our upstairs windows, hear the occasional rattle of machine guns and always assumed that they were the guns of our pilots. Aerial dogfights left trails of vapour and I can still picture a huge white figure of eight which seemed to hang over the Beckenham area in the still air of late summer for about 15 minutes after there were no more aircraft to be seen or heard.

We had three pear trees and a cooking apple tree in our garden. The tallest tree produced medium-sized sweet green pears which showed a red patch as they ripened. I was half way up that tree, about 30ft from the ground, as we neared midday on Sunday, September 15. Tony was up one of the other trees; the air raid warning had been sounded and we heard aircraft - a lot of aircraft. There they were, tight formations like black insects, high in the clear sky. At that height the aircrews would only have seen lines of suburban houses but when the bombs started falling it felt far more personal. Did they think we were scrumping? Tony and I descended rapidly from our respective trees and made for shelter via our upstairs kitchen. Mum had cooked and dished up the Sunday lunches; we picked up the plates, knives and forks, went back down the stairs and along to the Shipstone's basement without so much as slopping the gravy. Back at our home later in the day we could see, from our back windows looking towards London, thick clouds of distant smoke. Night fell, the smoke was underlit by a lurid red and the sirens sounded again as bombers returned to an easy mark.

In remembering the summer months of 1940, air raids come more easily to mind because they were immediate and noisy and gave actual glimpses of the enemy. To me, the threat of invasion was much more remote, although there were some thought-provoking moments such as seeing Ministry of Information leaflets urging everyone to "Stay Put" and being told why BBC newsreaders now gave their names at the start of each bulletin. The voices of Alvar Liddell, Bruce Belfrage and Frank Phillips became familiar to everyone and, as my father explained to me, “If you suddenly hear someone saying ‘Here iss der news and ziss is Alfarr Leedle reading eet’ you will know that something is wrong.”

Dad was still working in News Buildings during the day and had also become an air raid warden, with a post in Upper Norwood. He was occasionally in charge of the brick-built surface shelter at the top of Anerley Hill, opposite the Crystal Palace Hotel. This shelter replaced a wooden building which for many years had been used by passengers waiting for trams and, latterly, trolley buses. People who did not have Andersons in their back gardens, or pedestrians who were unable to reach home during an air raid, could always use these substantial and angular-looking public shelters which had small ungated entrances, wooden slatted seats and - naturally - no windows. Courting couples found them especially handy.

The trouble with using public shelters during an air raid alert was the temptation to stand in the doorway during the time when everything seemed quiet. “If they come over, we can dodge back inside,” was the general idea. A soldier home on leave was doing that - and had been warned a couple of times by my father - in the Anerley Hill shelter when a small bomb, or perhaps an anti-aircraft shell which had failed to explode in the air, fell in the road about 30 yards away. It did very little actual damage but a splinter of metal hit the soldier in the abdomen. He was quite conscious and in good spirits when the ambulance took him to hospital but my father learned later that the young man had died.

With the arrival of dark evenings in the late autumn we settled into a regular routine of waiting for the sirens, then heading downstairs and along the road to the basement flat of the ever-patient Mrs Shipstone and her kids, Dennis and Beryl. The Goldsmith clan of Mum, Tony, Margaret and I made it a total of seven; then we were joined by the tenants of the top flat at 13 Thicket Road, Mr and Mrs Frost and their baby. Mr Frost was a young man who worked as a projectionist at the Kings Hall Cinema in Penge and in the long hours of waiting for the single-note "all clear" siren would relate the basic plots of whatever films he was showing that week. He didn't think much of the sloppy romances but became quite colourful in his description of cops and robbers. "...then the 'ero comes in and finds out that his girlfriend has been threatened; then the shitbag comes in and they have a fight and the shitbag gets thrown out of the window. Then the 'ero decides to…" To Mr Frost (I can't remember his first name) most worthwhile films were a matter of 'eroes versus shitbags.

We spent more and more late hours in that basement and finally slept there as well, with Dennis, Beryl, Tony and me on makeshift beds - cushions on the floor served as mattresses. There were some proper beds, for Mrs Shipstone in the main front room and for Mum and Dad in a small bedroom which they shared with Margaret, who slept in a cot. In the time between an alert sounding and the all clear - if we youngsters were still awake - we would hear irregular anti-aircraft gunfire, increasing in volume as the drone of planes drew nearer; then fading when the raiders moved on. Even if aircraft could not be heard, there always seemed to be one or two distant guns in action, setting a strange echoing noise rolling among the houses followed by a throaty crump-crump as shells exploded in the sky.

Dad was not always with us because of his duties as a warden. In any case, he would never turn up until late, usually when we youngsters were asleep, and would be gone in the morning. By 7.30am, Mum and Margaret were usually back in our top flat, while Tony and I would get up, dress, and tidy away our bedding before venturing along to 19 Thicket road, keeping an eye open for any lumps of shrapnel. Collecting pieces of anti-aircraft shells became a new hobby, and, though I found some large chunks of ragged metal, I never came across what most kids prized - the nose end of a shell complete with brass rings showing the figures by which the timing mechanism had been set. A point of explanation here: the height at which an anti-aircraft shell exploded was determined by a timing device. The height of the planes at which they were being fired had to be worked out by one part of the gun crew and the timing ring on each shell set in accordance with instructions. The final link was the loading and firing of the shell. Ground-to-air guided missiles were at that time a distant dream - or a distant nightmare if you happened to be an aviator.

Into October, November, and December the raids went on - not every night but often enough to disrupt everyone's lives. When bombers came our way they were making for central London as their main target but would also drop their high explosive on the suburbs. The swoosh of falling bombs became familiar but always unnerving even though it was said that if you could hear it coming you were all right. In walking around Penge, Anerley, and Upper Norwood we had seen plenty of bomb-damaged houses, and many of the three-storey dwellings had whole side or front walls missing, leaving upper rooms exposed as though someone had opened up a giant dolls' house. Furniture could be still in place, with pictures and mirrors undisturbed on walls while at ground level was a mess of rubble, splintered wood, and battered domestic belongings.

There were stories of lucky escapes and unlucky tragedies in which the difference was only a matter of a few seconds. Cinemas were obliged to inform audiences if an air raid warning had been sounded - but most stayed seated while the film show continued. A few yards from the Odeon in Penge one night early in November, a bomb fell in the road while the patrons were standing as the national anthem was played at the end of the show. The audience was shaken but, luckily, unhurt; not so the man who had sneaked out a minute or so before the anthem and was blown fatally through a window of the Co-op department store.

As one wag remarked at the time, "What a dreadful way to die. I mean...*the Co-op.*"

There were, however, moments of non-gallows humour during the blitz. In full air raid warden rig of overalls, wellington boots, and steel helmet, Dad spent a busy part of one dark night extinguishing incendiary bombs which had fallen among buildings at Crystal Palace Parade. Some were in the grounds of the house occupied by Sid Legge, secretary of the Crystal Palace Company, so Dad scrambled over a wall - and landed in the middle of a garden cold frame. He stepped out of the broken glass and carried on dealing with the incendiaries. Later Sid Legge complained about the damage and was told that the breakage must have been caused by a bomb. "If it was, the bomb was wearing gumboots," said Sid.

Among the wardens at Dad's post was a tubby little tailor named Harry Kibble, who occasionally joined Dad on night patrols, ensuring that no householders were breaking the blackout regulations. They were doing this one November night when sirens sounded, anti-aircraft guns began firing, and pieces of shrapnel started clattering on roofs and hitting the roadway. The two men were wearing steel helmets, but there was no point in taking unnecessary risks, and Dad led the way to a substantial-looking horse chestnut with thickly protective lower branches. The wardens stood with their backs pressed against the tree trunk until the guns stopped firing and Dad deemed it safe to continue patrolling. As they walked away, Harry looked back and declared, "That tree wasn't any good - it's got no leaves on it!"

For many weeks, our homes in Thicket Road escaped any damage at all - not so much as a broken window - but that came to a sudden end one dark evening in October or November when half a dozen assorted Shipstones and Goldsmiths were in the back kitchen at number 13a, listening to the radio and enjoying Arthur Askey singing a jaunty little song which contained lines like "Take cover, take cover, the raiders are over..." We never heard the end of the song; there was an explosion, louder and closer than anything we had ever heard before. The kitchen window shattered behind the blackout curtains which billowed into the room, letting in bits of glass, dust, and a strange, acrid smell. Our instant reaction was to get out of the kitchen and into the windowless passageway which connected all the flat's rooms. The immediate danger seemed to be past, but the shock and puzzlement remained, and six-year-old Beryl, bless her, was crying. Mum checked on Margaret in her cot and she was undisturbed, even though the window in her room had disappeared.

A wall in the alleyway between the houses divided the entrance door of 13a from the door of neighbouring 15a, and we could hear its occupant, Miss Hughes, an apparently eternal spinster, screaming hysterically: "Where are the wardens? Where are the wardens?" Mum glanced contemptuously towards the source of the noise. "What does she expect the wardens to do? Stick her bloody windows back together again?"

As we saw in the morning, the bomb had destroyed a house on the corner of Versailles Road and Anerley Road, less than 200 yards away. Within an hour of the bomb falling, the mess inside the Shipstone's flat had been cleared up, the ragged blackout curtains had beeen repaired, and we eventually settled down for a night with more than the usual supply of fresh air. Three-year-old Margaret awoke in her cot during the small hours and sensed that all was not well. "Mum!" she called to the figure in the nearby bed, "has that Hitler bombed us?"

CHAPTER 4 - HAIRY TIME IN EXETER

Yes, Hitler had bombed - and would continue to bomb - us occasionally, and even when German aircraft were not actually dropping explosives, they would still be overhead, sometimes two or three nights a week, and there was the expectation that the next bomb could be closer than the one that interrupted Arthur Askey's song. Families who had been "bombed out" of their homes in other parts of the locality arrived to take over empty accommodation in our road. Three people from Parish Lane in Penge appeared in what we called "the hall flat" - the one above the basement - at 19 Thicket Road and stayed for a month until their other home had been repaired.

On most evenings at home the radio would be tuned in to either the "Home" or "Forces" programme (I will explain the terms in a moment) in the hope of listening to comedy shows with people like Nan Kenway and Douglas Young. Kenway was the sensible one while Young affected to mishear whatever she was saying and turn it to the subject of food. For example, if Nan Kenway mentioned that a friend was suffering from frightful bunions, Douglas Young would say in his deeply distracted way, "I likes that." "You like what?" his partner would ask. "Tripe and onions," would come the reply. Pause for laughter from studio audience. "Dished up with some bread and butter or a few vegetables - very tasty...very sweet." The "very tasty...very sweet" part became one of the many catchphrases generated by the radio and taken up by the general public. If someone gave you a biscuit you would, at the first bite, say "very tasty... very sweet" and that would raise a smile. Possibly the greatest generator of catchphrases was Tommy Handley's programme ITMA, of which more later.

"Home" and "Forces" stations on the radio? They were introduced early in the war, with the former providing more serious programmes, including the now increased number of daily news bulletins, discussions and plays. The latter, which replaced the pre-war regional services, concentrated on light entertainment - music by dance bands with guest singers, and comedy programmes.

For listeners like us in the London area, the evening radio programmes also provided an unofficial early warning system for air raids. In our top flat we would be getting normal reception on the long wave and then quite suddenly almost lose the programme. Volume would drop and there would be a strange echoing element in the sound. It was undoubtedly the same programme but with such a poor signal that it was hardly worth the trouble of trying to hear it. Within a quarter of an hour the air raid sirens would start, we would look at each other and say, "They're on the way again" - and prepare to leave for a safer level. It was a long time later that the link between the poor radio reception and the German bombers was explained. A strong signal broadcast from London was a useful guide for any incoming aircraft, so when approaching raiders were detected some distance away the powerful transmitters were switched off and BBC programmes continued on lower power from stations away from the capital.

We also found out later that the Germans were developing a radio signal beamed from their side of the Channel in order to guide the bombers and that the British had worked out ways of rendering it useless. In late 1940, however, all we knew was that if Nan Kenway and Douglas Young, among others, could not be heard then it was time to get moving. On the couple of occasions we did not move quickly enough and were caught in the top flat as bombs fell up to a mile away, the effect on the building was alarming. It was necessary to stand with feet apart as the structure quite literally swayed for a few seconds. Once it had stopped, we scooted downstairs.

During the day our schooling continued, but the idea of starting and finishing early was discontinued as the approach of winter brought darker mornings. The National Savings movement ("Lend to Defend the Right to be Free!" said the posters) became part of school life with teachers collecting the money. Few of us actually achieved the aim of having enough for a savings certificate, which cost fifteen shillings, but a girl called Nellie Moore, of Lullington Road, managed it. Mr Macleod saw this as a practical way of illustrating his lessons in arithmetic and simple interest. "She is now like a little bank," he said, which puzzled some of us because the girl looked nothing like a brown sandstone building.

The teacher continued that the fifteen shillings was now earning interest at the rate of two-and-a-half per cent and that in ten years' time her certificate would be worth a pound and sixpence. None of the class had the gumption or nerve to inquire whether the purchasing power of a pound and sixpence in the distant 1950 would be anything like what you could get for fifteen shillings in the present 1940.

The dishing out of mid-morning school milk continued except that there was a temporary shortage of bottles containing a third of a pint. For a while the classes received their milk in individual china beakers filled from quart bottles, and for some mysterious reason, the job of pouring it was given to me and a scruffy but well-meaning girl who lived in Ridsdale Road. On November mornings, in some sort of unheated ante-room, we were faced with substantial bottles and trays of empty beakers into which we tried to tip equal amounts. We wore no extra clothing to protect the milk from us or us from the milk. The room, our hands and especially the bottles were very cold. There were occasional crises as we either poured too much or too little, or the headmaster Frank Copp came to see how we were getting along. While we coped with all this the girl, I noticed, gradually turned into a nine-year-old replica of what her mother must have been like. She already had the verbal repertoire - "You can't be too fussy these days" and "We'll just have to make the best of it" - while her shoulders became protectively hunched in the way of women we had seen waiting in queues or pushing their way through crowds at Maple Road market. I was glad when the little bottles returned. Heaven only knows what a health inspector would have made of the previous arrangement.

On the broader front we already knew that back in June the slightly comic dictator Mussolini had brought Italy into the war against us and now, in November, had attacked Greece, albeit with no great success. We were also cheered by the Fleet Air Arm raid which crippled the Italian fleet at Taranto. The news seemed to be about a mixture of air raids on cities like Coventry, Bristol, and London, with other stories about armed fighting in what to ordinary people were remote places such as Albania, Sidi Barani, and Tobruk. But as the London bombing continued - and with it the danger to those in the suburbs - there was talk of evacuation, which for Tony and I became a reality in January 1941. It was not compulsory, so Dennis and Beryl Shipstone remained with their mother, but large numbers of other schoolchildren from Penge and Anerley, plus many of their teachers, headed west.

There have been numerous books and television documentaries - even a stage play turned into a film called "No Room at the Inn" - about evacuees. Exactly how it was and the effect on those who were sent off to supposedly safe places away from London depended on many different factors, the most important and the most unpredictable being human nature. To give one example: when our family spent a holiday with Aunt Rose, Uncle

Tom, and Geoff at Folkestone in 1939, they did not have enough sleeping accommodation, so Tony and I spent each night with their next-door neighbours. They were a charming young couple, childless and with a neat and comfortable home into which we were given the friendliest of welcomes. A few months later they provided a home for two evacuees - and not long after that appeared in court for ill-treating them, among the exhibits being a short, thick stick with which the children had been repeatedly beaten. There were, of course, no headlines about evacuees who settled in well and caused, or were not caused, any trouble - so we'll go ahead with how it worked out for me and Tony.

I cannot remember the date, but it was a very dark and cold morning in January 1941, and we were both due at our respective schools by eight o'clock. Tony had to be at the Beckenham Technical College, so left home around seven in order to walk down to the bus stop at the Crooked Billet pub and catch the 227 single decker bus. Mum took me down to Anerley Junior School and seemed very subdued as we joined the throng of parents and kids walking through the gloom. I carried a small canvas satchel - bought by Mum from the market in Maple Road - containing spare socks, a change of underwear, towel, face flannel and soap. Tony must have had something similar. We had no idea where we would be going but Mum had said that it would be nice if we went to Devon. The school hall was crowded and buzzing with rumours, but one of the teachers confirmed that it would be Devon, probably Exeter, and then it all quietened down as lists of names were called out and kids said goodbye to parents. There were surprisingly few tears.

Mum kissed me on the cheek, I stepped forward with several others from my class, and when I looked back Mum had gone. We were taken outside, herded on to red London double decker buses, and set off up Anerley Hill. Some of the kids started singing songs that were unfamiliar to me - "Daisy Bell" and "She Was a Dear Little Dicky Bird" - which must have been those sung by their families at parties or on outings. The sun came out as the bus took us through London, past some of the sights I remembered from the school outing to the zoo about eighteen months previously. We arrived at Paddington station, were put onto a train. While we waited, photographers took pictures of children waving from carriage windows. I was looking for Tony and eventually caught sight of him, but he was with friends of his own age and from the technical college.

We were, I think, given some sandwiches and a drink before the train pulled out. Previous rail journeys for me had been comparatively short trips from East Croydon to Eastbourne, so this one appeared to go on for a long time and passed through seemingly endless tracts of countryside. It was the late afternoon when we arrived at Exeter. Again, no sign of Tony, but I was with boys from my class at school as we were taken to some sort of hostel, fed - the bread pudding was very popular - and washed before being sent to bed in long rooms like hospital wards.

We woke to find that it had snowed overnight and after breakfast there was a long wait while some of the teachers from Anerley called out names of various children who were then taken off - presumably to their foster parents.

In the years since that time, I have heard and read about evacuees who arrived at their destination and stood around while potential carers looked at them as though they were in some sort of slave market and made their choice on the basis of suitability for helping around the house or, in some cases, around the farm. This was not my experience. My name was called and I was taken out to a car which contained Tony. He asked if I was all right and we chatted as the driver and a teacher took us through the snow-covered streets of Exeter, eventually stopping outside a hairdresser's shop at 145 Sidwell Street. We were taken inside and introduced to Mrs Newberry, a middle-aged lady who ran the hairdresser's with the aid of her two daughters and another girl assistant. Mrs Newberry, our foster mother, took us to a waiting room at the back of the shop where we sat on a large settee - I think it may have been a Put-U-Up - while she attended to customers.

We must have had lunch at some time, although I cannot remember it. Customers who shared the settee while they waited were interested in hearing about our blitz experiences, which I have to confess grew more colourful in the telling. When there were no customers to entertain, we read magazines of which there were plenty, most of them - like Picturegoer - devoted to the film industry, its stars, and their latest releases. Finally, at around six o'clock, the last customer disappeared into the dark streets; it was time for the shop to close and the Newberrys - mother and two daughters, plus a Scottie dog called Cinders and their two evacuees - prepared to depart for the family home on the other side of Exeter. We caught a bus which went past the Guildhall, across the river, and along Cowick Road to Broadway, where the bus turned round. Then it was a walk to 101 Cowick Hill, a detached house with - as I later found - a great view across the city with its prominent cathedral.

The family was given a twittering welcome; there, in various cages, were more than twenty budgerigars and at least one canary - and they all had individual names. As Tony and I took it all in we were shown to the front bedroom we would be sharing, put down our few belongings and returned downstairs just as Mr Newberry arrived home from his workplace, a chemist's shop not far from the cathedral.

So this was the family. Mrs Newberry was motherly, probably in her late 40s, and at the same time a pleasantly efficient and level-headed business lady; the elder daughter, Evelyn, was 18 and quite pretty; her sister, Hilda, was 15 and on her way to becoming a good-looking young lady. Mr Newberry, however, was something of a disappointment; he appeared to be much older than his wife, had a whining voice, and his demeanour was that of a born worrier. There was a son, Ken, away in the army, although we would meet him later. For the present, there was supper of baked beans on toast followed by a steaming mug of cocoa, and then it was time for bed.

The fact that Tony and I appeared to have two addresses - the shop at 145 Sidwell Street and the house at 101 Cowick Hill - was at first a puzzle to the education authorities as far as I was concerned. They wanted to send me to a junior school near the house until it was explained that the shop a couple of miles away would be the daytime address and I was enrolled at St Sidwell School, only a few minutes' walk from the salon. Tony went to the local equivalent of a technical school midway between the two addresses, meeting up with many of his Beckenham Tech friends, including one with the unlikely name of Dennis Germany, known to his classmates as Fritz. You couldn't make it up, but his mother's maiden name was England - really. More about Tony and Fritz later.

I got on very well with Mrs Newberry and her daughters. Evelyn and Hilda were absolutely crazy about the world of films, its stars and, in particular, Jeanette MacDonald and Nelson Eddy, who regularly sang their way through several reels of wafer-thin plots. Visiting the cinema was an essential part of the girls' lives, and with them I managed to see funny films like Chaplin's "The Great Dictator", colourful and thrilling ones such as "The Thief of Baghdad" and even sat through other features including "Wuthering Heights". Mrs Newberry took me to see "Jack and the Beanstalk" at the local theatre sometime in late January or early February because at that time most professional pantomimes ran from Boxing Day until well into the New Year.

Because of my age (I'd had my tenth birthday in December 1940) aided by what I can only label as a natural adaptability, life as an evacuee with my foster family was quite agreeable. I made friends, including a boy about my own age whose mother ran a shop a few doors further along Sidwell Street. Her husband was in the Royal Navy and their son was called Rodney, after a battleship. There was also a younger lad who lived with his widowed mother in one of the cottage-type places in Gaty Court, a passage which led down the side of the salon. There were also times when I would help out in the hairdresser's, donning a long white coat and sweeping up or sometimes wielding one of the hand-held dryers which came into use at busy times.

Tony, at 14, had different ideas and was already planning for adult life. Remember that many boys left school at 14 then, but the technical college provided the chance to learn more by staying on until 16 and Tony was developing his artistic ability there by designing and producing posters aimed at the war effort. Hoardings with huge colourful posters had long been an essential part of getting over a message in the days before commercial radio or television. Newspapers and magazines carried advertisements, of course, but there was no escaping the visual impact of larger-than-life reproductions of the two ragged-arsed Bisto Kids in their eye-closing ecstasy of smelling gravy made with brown powder, or the man happily clinging to a jar of yeast extract as it bobbed around in the middle of an ocean, secure in the knowledge that "Bovril Prevents That Sinking Feeling."

It was only natural that in wartime the great British public should be bombarded with messages to "Dig for Victory" while putting any spare cash into National Savings and being constantly aware that "Careless Talk Costs Lives". Many well-illustrated books have been produced about these campaigns. At a local level, there was scope for schoolchildren to win prizes of savings stamps by designing posters for the latest National Savings campaign - "Salute the Soldier Week", or "Wings for Victory". Our cluttered water colours were a puny contrast to the eye-catchingly rich use of poster colours used by boys at the technical college who were clever enough to take one well-illustrated idea and back it with a simple message.

Tony was good at coming up with ideas, then providing the design and illustration complete with appropriate lettering. He had never been short of confidence, and his success at college, together with the growing awareness of other things that boys of 14-plus acquire, widened the gap between us. He was particularly scathing when I, having sat through an exam I barely remembered, was deemed to have failed the dreaded eleven-plus. According to him, I would end up as a dustman - as refuse collectors were called in those days.

We had plenty of reminders that the war was never far away. There were occasional air raid warnings but no sign of activity, although Plymouth and Devonport were heavily bombed on the night of March 20. Still, there were no military targets in Exeter - or were there? One of my occasional tasks when I nipped back to the shop at lunchtime was to go a few doors up Sidwell Street to a baker's and buy hot Cornish pasties and a shilling's worth of cakes for Mrs Newberry, her two daughters, and a blonde girl called Doreen who also did shampoo and sets in the hairdresser's. Plus, of course, me and Tony - who did not always turn up. A couple of doors further along the road was a building with a large frontage which had all the appearance of having been a garage or extensive workshop. One day the door had been left half open and I looked inside to find an aircraft fuselage - Spitfire or Hurricane - being built. There was hardly time to take it all in before a shout from the back of the workshop sent me scurrying. I never saw the workshop door open again.

In April, about three months after we had been sent to Exeter, Tony returned to Anerley for a couple of weeks. I am not sure what prompted the visit but he returned with vivid stories of further bomb damage, and he had also witnessed the final destruction of the one remaining icon of the old Crystal Palace - the north tower. Following the fire of 1936, the towers had been the only reminder of the structure's glory days, and the south tower, with its base adjacent to Anerley Hill, was dismantled as war approached. Why the north tower was allowed to remain, providing a wonderful landmark for enemy aircraft on their way to London, is something of a mystery. However, in April of 1941, it was decided that there was sufficient room around the tower to bring it down with explosives. Newspapers carried pictures of the wreckage and prompted my own thoughts of the time I had paid twopence to climb what seemed like endless flights of stairs to the viewing gallery to look across the south eastern counties of Kent and Surrey or turn north to see over the sprawl of London, beyond the dome of St Paul's to the other palace - Alexandra. Now the 282-foot tower had gone for ever.

Mr Newberry continued to be something of a puzzle - negative in his general attitude and unsure about things to which most people would never give a second thought. If the radio was switched off at the end of a programme he would not allow it to be turned on again for half an hour. The valves, he said, had to be allowed to cool down properly because they might otherwise be damaged. Fortunately this little restriction did not interfere with what to me and many others would have been the listening highlights of Sunday - "Hi, Gang!" with Ben Lyon, Bebe Daniels and Vic Oliver in the afternoon followed in the evening by "Happidrome". He never talked about it, but Mr Newberry had, I think, been an officer in the Royal Navy during the First World War. One of the few times I saw him badly affected by war news was on May 24 1941, when a BBC news bulletin announced the sinking of HMS Hood in the Atlantic. The battleship had exploded while taking on the Bismarck, newest of the German fleet, but its triumph was short lived and it, too, was destroyed three days later.

As spring gave way to summer we had a few Sunday excursions by train from Exeter to the coast at Dawlish and Dawlish Warren, that fascinating part of the western railway network which runs next to the coast itself. At that time, the sands of Dawlish Warren stretched out in a long series of dunes and tough, spiky grass between the line and the sea. One Sunday in June I was there with Hilda and Doreen, got horribly sunburned, and returned to Cowick Hill to find Mrs Newberry upset that we "had been enjoying ourselves when those poor Russians were being attacked by Hitler." It was June 22, and I doubt if many people up to that time had ever thought about Russia other than as a cold and mysterious place which, in the early months of the war, was solely concerned with attacking the equally cold and mysterious Finland.

At St Sidwell School I was now in the class from which, in a couple of months, I was due to leave and go to a different place for seniors in another part of the city. Schooling at that time was not as heavily punctuated with tests and assessments as education would eventually become; in fact, I cannot remember any form of testing while I was there. With an effort, I can recall that the headmaster at St Sidwell was a Mr Harris and that the school's only modern feature was its use of a radio programme once a week to teach musical appreciation. In my case, it succeeded. There was also one notable occasion when it was discovered that I was the only boy in the class who knew how to spell "government." The teacher at that time was a young man who shortly afterwards left to join the Royal Air Force and we all wished him "Cheerio - and happy landings." He wanted to be aircrew and I sometimes wonder if he survived.

While more people joined the armed forces, at least one managed - in the phrase of the time - to "work his ticket." This was Ken Newberry, eldest child and only son, who left the army and came home to his family in an increasingly crowded house at Cowick Hill where he slept in a camp bed on the landing. Tony felt that he and I should return to Anerley and I don't know whether this was prompted by the new set-up in our foster home, matters affecting his own schooling, or the reduced danger to London since Germany started concentrating its war effort against Russia. In any case, I had no say in the matter. Tony made a phone call to the place where our father worked and, because Dad was not there at the time, left a message that we would be returning the following day.

Our belongings were put together in an assortment of parcels and bags, and the next morning we left the Newberry family, walking down the front steps of 101 Cowick Hill for the last time. We caught a bus into Exeter, found the coach station, and headed for London on what seemed to be a long, hot journey with one break for a cup of tea. On one long, straight section of the Great West

Road with no buildings on either side, I noticed concrete pillars at regular intervals and was told that they had been erected at the time of the invasion scare to prevent the road being used by the Germans as a landing strip. We struggled with our luggage from the Victoria coach station to the nearby railway terminus and eventually caught a train to the Crystal Palace Low Level.

How much this had all cost and where Tony got the money is still a mystery to me, but he had organised it all - and there we were making our way down Anerley Road and into Thicket Road where Dennis and Beryl Shipstone were playing outside number 13. We walked past, turned in at the gate of number 19, and climbed the familiar stairs to the top flat. Mum and Margaret were in the kitchen and the look on Mum's face said it all as we walked in; the previous night's phone message had obviously not been delivered.

While that last sentence is true and provides what would have been a glib ending to this chapter, I must take this late - very late - opportunity to acknowledge the kindness of the Newberrys in taking care of Tony and me for more than seven months. I did not write to thank them, and I don't know if anyone else thought to let our foster family know that we had arrived home safely.

It must have been August 1941 when Tony and I left Exeter. In April the following year the city was the first on the list of heavy so-called Baedeker raids by the Luftwaffe. Angered by the RAF's increasing night campaign over Germany, Hitler ordered reprisals against cities with large civilian populations and began hitting, in turn, Exeter, Bath, Norwich, York, Grimsby and Canterbury over a period of a few weeks. These concentrated attacks, it was noticed, were on places in a travellers' guidebook first produced in the 19th century by the German publisher Karl Baedeker - hence the name given to the campaign.

The city of Exeter was initially raided on the nights of April 23 and 24. On the first occasion, 45 aircraft took part, but because of cloud, only a few found the target. Bombing was scattered, killing 13 people, injuring eight, and damaging 200 houses. The following night 60 aircraft took part in a two-wave assault which killed 80 and injured 55. German claims were that, in addition to incendiary bombs, 175 tonnes of high explosive had been dropped on the city, but British estimates scaled this down to a total of 28 tonnes over the two nights. The Luftwaffe had not finished with Exeter; it was hit again on May 3 when 163 people were killed, 131 seriously injured, and much of the city's historic centre was razed by fire.

There was, apparently, little or no effect on the house at 101 Cowick Hill but a large part of Sidwell Street, including the hairdresser's at 145, was battered beyond recognition and has since been completely rebuilt without the peculiar little alleyway I knew as Gaty Court. None of the Newberrys would have been in their shop at night, but I wonder what happened to the woman - a troubled soul at the best of times - who lived in the upstairs flat, to Rodney and his mother nearby, and to the tenants who occupied the strange, near-Dickensian dwellings of Gaty Court. I also wonder who decided that Exeter would be a safe place for evacuees.

CHAPTER 5 - JUGGLING WITH FIVE BOOKS

Being at home again seemed strange for all sorts of reasons. Having overcome their surprise at our sudden appearance, Mum and four-year-old Margaret were pleased to see Tony and me. Tony did all the explaining - whatever it was - and it was he who had the job of finding Dad, then telling it all again. It was late in the day but thanks to Double Summer Time there was still plenty of daylight left for him to find Dad at the allotment. It was my turn to be surprised. The family had taken the Dig for Victory campaign to heart and was tending one of the many patches of land marked out by the local council just the other side of the wall from Anerley Junior School. Dad, who had never shown the slightest interest in growing anything in our back garden, was now taming an area of about 25 feet by 40 feet and planting vegetables. When he came home later he did not seem particularly pleased at being reunited with his two sons, which may sound harsh, but there were factors of which I was not aware.

As I found out many years later, at the time Tony and I went to Exeter things between Mum and Dad were far from ideal and on at least one occasion this had led to physical violence against my mother. Dad was hail-fellow-well-met and an erudite discussion leader among his many acquaintances on the weekend round of pubs around Penge, Anerley and Upper Norwood but felt that he was missing the opportunities his first-class brain should have offered. He was also a near-hopeless case when it came to handling money. His salary as assistant editor of a large group of local newspapers was much larger than average, but far too much of it went over pub counters. Apart from this, other women found him attractive and probably provided opportunities at the end of which he would return to his wife and three kids in a 12s 6d-a-week flat which had only the most basic essentials. At 37 years of age, he was stuck in a rut - and there was also a war which appeared to be going badly and in which he could take no active, full-time part. To be fair, he would occasionally become the sort of father that any kid would be proud of, but there were too many times when he would retreat into a black, uncommunicative mood in which we would be glad to let him have the main room to himself while we sat in the kitchen or went out to find our friends.,

The flat to which Tony and I returned had not changed in seven months, but in the meantime I at least had grown used to living in a well-furnished house with a separate bathroom containing facilities for washing in hot water which came from a tap and cleaning one's teeth without the rest of the household looking on. Now we were back to kitchen-based living, with the flat's sole cold tap over a deep sink. Hot water came from a kettle heated on the nearby gas stove and poured into an enamel basin. The bath was also in the kitchen and covered by tongue-and-groove boarding; once a week the cover was removed and hot water provided by a temperamental gas-powered geyser which gave out a loud explosion if anyone other than my mother tried to light it.

All the same, I was pleased to be home and was soon catching up with old friends as well as getting to know new people who had moved into our end of Thicket Road. The Shipstones were still in the basement at number 13a and the Hughes family had remained opposite us at 10; Ian Robinson and his brother Stuart had not returned from Exeter (I had seen them a couple of times when I was down there) but Mr White, our milkman who lived downstairs at number 8, was still there with his wife and three children, including Betty who was about my age. Newcomers included Roy Caller, also about my age, whose family had moved into the hall-floor flat next door to us at number 21.

Tony resumed his education at Beckenham Tech, joined by Dennis Germany, also back from Exeter. They continued to produce outstanding artwork, still with the emphasis on posters, and both had examples on show at the Royal Academy when it staged a special exhibition of National Savings posters designed and painted by pupils from colleges across the country. Tony and "Fritz" were duly featured in an article in the Penge and Anerley News which included photographs of them and their exhibits. The poster by Tony showed a large money box with an open door from which was emerging a military tank, complete with gun turret, while bold text confirmed the message about savings - "T'anks for Your Pennies." I cannot recall the exact wording on the piece by "Fritz" but the illustration included cog wheels fed from above by lubricant from an oilcan. The drops of oil turned into coins as they met the wheels of industry and became bombs as they dropped out. There must have been many similar posters in the exhibition and there were no prizes for the young artists apart from the kudos of being able to say that their work had been on show at the Royal Academy. For Tony, it was the first of several designs and illustrations which came frustratingly close to earning him recognition.

A little further up Thicket Road, at number 4, lived a teenage girl who was staying there with her uncle's family. Daphne Crabbe had survived the bombing of her previous home in nearby Anerley Park and I am not sure if she had been orphaned by the incident or whether her parents had moved away, leaving their daughter in the care of relatives in order to complete her education at the Beckenham High School for Girls. Daphne Crabbe was friends with Joyce Hughes, who attended the same school and would shortly be joined there by her young sister Gwen. Over the next couple of years, we would get to know and like the rather lumpy Daphne, who liked to share her problems with our mother.

Mum, however, had problems of her own - mainly to do with health. Not long after our return, she developed phlebitis and spent three weeks in hospital at Farnborough, on the far side of Bromley. Mrs Shipstone, ever the good neighbour, took Margaret and me into her home, leaving Tony and Dad to fend for themselves in the top flat. For as long as I could remember, Mum had been troubled by varicose veins in her legs. When the inflammation flared up it caused her so much pain that she could barely walk - and there was a lot of walking to do in those times of no domestic refrigerators. Setting off with a wicker basket was necessary on most days and even the shortest trip meant going up a steep stretch of Anerley Road, carrying the shopping back and then climbing more than 50 steps and stairs to the flat. Her spell in hospital was also an alarm call for Dad who was noticeably more considerate - even affectionate - towards Mum when she returned home.

I was still staying with Mrs Shipstone when school summer holidays ended. On the last Sunday afternoon, I went to the Rialto cinema in Church Road, Upper Norwood, and saw Cary Grant and Irene Dunne in "Penny Serenade" and remember walking back down Anerley Hill, wondering whether I would resume school at Anerley Junior or be sent to the senior school in Oakfield Road. Dennis Shipstone, who had turned 11 in June, was due to join the seniors but my birthday was not until December and it turned out that this gave me a last few weeks with the juniors. Len Quinnell, not 11 until September, was also among my classmates during a term which included the Great Coke Fight and a lecture by a Norwegian naval officer.

Coke, in those days, was nothing to do with either the soft drinks industry or the drugs trade. It was boiler fuel which came in black lumps about half the size of a man's fist and was surprisingly light. Going again into history, it has to be explained that domestic gas at that time was produced from coal mined in Britain and heat-treated at the many gas works around the country. Once the gas and other by-products had been extracted, what remained was coke - still useable as fuel provided it had a plentiful supply of oxygen. The boilers which heated Anerley school were designed to burn coke and there was a large supply of the stuff heaped in one corner of the playground. Going anywhere near it was strictly forbidden, of course, so it was a mystery to everyone when at playtime one afternoon the air was suddenly thick with lumps flying in all directions. I can honestly say that I was not involved and did not know who cast the first coke-stone or what had started it all. Hostilities lasted less than a minute but that was enough to turn what had been an orderly pile of fuel into scattered remnants which took the long-suffering caretaker a couple of hours to restore.

When everyone was back in their classrooms, headmaster Mr Jack Copp did the rounds in an effort to find the culprits. Naturally, nobody knew anything and I have a vivid memory of his standing just inside the door of the top class and, having been assured by us that we were all innocent, his look across the room to where a boy called Derek Walker sat. "Do you know anything about it, Walker?" asked the head. Derek, whose parents ran an off-licence near the school, was the picture of curly-haired innocence - apart from sporting a recently-acquired huge multi-coloured lump on his forehead. He looked back at

Mr Copp. “No, sir,” he said. And that was it; Mr Copp just turned and left.

The Norwegian naval officer appeared one day when the whole school was assembled in the main hall. We were all impressed by his uniform as he stood on the stage; then he introduced himself and started to talk about the German invasion of Denmark and Norway - but in a humorous and slightly mocking way. This was a change from some of the horror stories we had heard. He talked about the German troops who occupied Denmark treating it as some sort of holiday resort and having to alter the size of their uniforms as they grew fat on its butter and bacon. In Norway there had been all kinds of resistance, including pranks by children who in their own small way had learned to make life uncomfortable for the invaders. Finally he talked about his own escape from Norway and the elaborate arrangements which led to his voyage with several other men across the North Sea in a fishing boat with the tense first few miles as they avoided German coastal patrols.

We all enjoyed the talk given by our Scandinavian visitor and, of course, had to write a composition (essay, in modern terms) about it. Propaganda? Of course it was - but the country was at war and, although the Battle of Britain had been a year ago, we were still far from safe. German forces appeared to be capturing Russian cities, apart from Moscow; U-boats were sinking an increasing number of ships in the transatlantic convoys we relied on for food and war materials; and one of our aircraft carriers, the Ark Royal, had also been sunk.

The significance of Japan's attack on Pearl Harbour on December 6 was not fully grasped by most junior school children in England. At the time, it just confirmed that anything with "Made in Japan" stamped on it was not to be trusted - and wasn't America already on our side, anyway? After all, Gary Cooper had already shot plenty of Germans in the 1941 production of "Sergeant York" and, although that was a story about the First World War, it showed where Hollywood's sympathies lay. News from the Pacific, however, was anything but pacifying - British battleships Repulse and Prince of Wales sunk by the Japanese who were also occupying islands and territories in what appeared to be an unstoppable succession of victories.

Mum had been back with us since mid-September of 1941, and we were all much more conscious of the need to help by running errands and going to the shops while she recovered her mobility. For her, and indeed for millions of other Mums, there was an increasing strain of feeding families by producing meals at a time when more and more commodities were either rationed or in short supply. Everyone had a ration book, issued each year by the Ministry of Food. These contained pages of coupons, some in different colours, set out in a week-by-week format. For those items already rationed, the pages would be designated - bacon, butter, sugar, meat, tea, margarine, jam, cheese, eggs, clothes and coal. There were spare, untitled pages - hence the colours - for things likely to be rationed, and it was anybody's guess as to which of these would be next. Rice, dried fruit, soap, tinned tomatoes, and peas, as well as sweets and biscuits would all become rationed during 1942.

As keeper of the family's ration books, Mum also had to make sure that we were registered for our supplies and this meant choosing one particular grocer, one butcher, and one coal merchant from the shops in our locality. This at least meant that we were sure of getting our rationed goods; it also helped if a shop's registered customer wanted something that was not rationed but was simply in short supply. Anyone recognised as not being among the registered customers was likely to be told that the shop had sold out of whatever unrationed item they were seeking. So, visiting the grocer often became a game of finding out if they had anything extra "under the counter." We are, of course, talking of a presupermarket time when customers were dealt with individually by an assistant who, in addition to counting up purchases in shillings and pence without a calculator, had to be handed one or more of the customers' ration books. Coupons for the items - also marked in appropriate quantities - were then either heavily crossed out with indelible pencil (no ballpoints yet) or clipped out with scissors. An additional thought: you may have been entitled to some foodstuffs but you still had to pay for them!

A further complication arrived in December of 1941, when points rationing was introduced. Pages marked out with squares headed "Points" had been part of ration books for some time; then it was announced that these were to be used for a variety of previously unrationed goods, particularly tinned food. Each person was allocated a certain number of points per month, and the number required per item varied according to its size and availability. A small tin of salmon, I remember, needed 32 points and would have wiped out a month's allocation; better to stick with something less punitive, like baked beans.

Mums everywhere also had to cope with queues, not just of a dozen people but long, out-of-the-shop-door-and-along-the-street lines of women with shopping baskets, inching forward. Waiting - for what? It was said jokingly (but most jokes have a grain of truth) that if you saw a queue it was best to join it straight away and then find out what was likely to be at the other end. Time for the joke about the old lady who inadvertently joined a theatre queue and was told that it was for "Tales of Hoffman." Her comment: "Well, you can't be too fussy about what you eat these days." There were occasionally some strange items, particularly at the fishmonger's, but perfectly ordinary commodities could unaccountably acquire a rarity value merely by being in short supply. "If all the onions in Penge were placed together, there would be a hell of a scramble for both of them," said a line in The Penguin Column which my father wrote each week in the "Penge and Anerley News."

The greengrocer's - Mum usually went to Burley's in Anerley Road - was one shop where, for basic vegetables, no book was needed, although "only 2lbs per customer" restrictions could be temporarily applied for something like carrots. You could also go to the baker's and pick up a grey-looking loaf without having to worry about coupons or points. Food Minister Lord Woolton had said, "Fill 'em up with bread and potatoes" when referring to children, but the same also applied to many others.

So, the daily routine of shopping for the family's needs, juggling the ration books and money, as well as coping with queues, was something for which most mothers deserved a medal. The majority managed in their own way without resorting to all those well-meant but often laughable ideas put forward in radio programmes like "The Kitchen Front" (Freddie Grizewood and Mabel Constanduros were among the early-morning voices) and Ministry of Food recipes including Woolton Pie - a vegetable concoction which nobody that I knew ever attempted. And "How to make mock duck" - they must have been joking; even when times were supposed to have been good, most of us had never even tasted *real* duck. At the cinema there were instant hints in a series called "Food Flash" - announced with a bomb-burst optical and clash of cymbals - which patrons forgot as soon as the big picture came on. And in church halls across the country, upper crust old biddies in funny hats and sensible shoes were dishing out advisory leaflets and saying "You must learn to *economise*" to women who for years had known all about bringing up large families on next to bugger-all.

In cafes and restaurants there was no rationing. You could have a meal without the need to produce a coupon of any sort so, if you were rich enough, the regulations could be by-passed. This anomaly was acknowledged in some towns by the opening of civic restaurants, subsidised by the local authority and offering rather basic meals at a cut price. There was one opposite The Alma pub in Church Road, Upper Norwood, which I visited a few times with Mum and Margaret while on shopping trips. The routine was to pay at a cash desk first and take your ticket, with a tray, to the long serving hatch and where women would put your order onto a plate. The business of then finding an unoccupied and uncluttered table was much the same then as it is now in fast food places; some things never change.

The civic restaurant served meat and veg, with the emphasis on the latter and there was one occasion when Margaret complained to Mum and me that she had no meat at all. Mum had a look, picked up the plate and headed for the serving hatch. A minute later she was back with a bemused expression on her face. "There is some meat," she said. "Look - it's under that potato." (A pause while I wipe my eyes; I still don't know whether to laugh or cry.) For younger children the restaurant provided plates with a picture and Margaret has since admitted that she only ate the food in order to see what picture had been concealed by the veg, gravy, and miniscule meat.

The other all-important food to escape rationing was fish and chips - a combination so dear to the hearts of the British that one would never write the more grammatically correct "*were* fish and chips". The partnership, created long ago in some steamy, greasy heaven, played its wartime role by providing meals wrapped in newspaper and cooked in shops which on dark nights were havens of light, warmth, and expectation. Waiting your turn to be served was part of the ritual - revelling in the smell and sizzle of hot fat, watching the proprietor's dexterity with those wire scoops, feeling the warmth of the food through the tightly-wrapped bundle (if you were taking it home) and then, having negotiated the blackout curtains, getting used to the pitch blackness of the street outside. In a wider sense, fish and chips not only helped to preserve the British way of life, it also won the hearts of many servicemen and women who were trying it for the first time far from their overseas homes.

So, we headed into 1942, and I cannot recall much news of the family beyond our immediate circle. At some time we received from Uncle Dan in India, a bulky package containing a slice of wedding cake. "Huh!" said Mum, "He always was a fool about marriage" - a remark which intrigued me because I thought, quite correctly, that Dan had not been married before. We each enjoyed a few crumbs of the cake. There were no visits from aunts or uncles, but we did know that Uncle Jim had split from his wife, Elsie, and wondered how that affected their children, Lawrence and Audrey. As far as others, particularly those in the Eastbourne area, were concerned, it was assumed that no news was good news. There would have to be a lot of catching up at some time in the future.

Going back to school at the start of 1942 meant that my time with Anerley Junior Mixed was over and I would have to start at the boys-only building in Oakfield Road, Penge. The infants and junior schools had been fairly modern, single-storey places which felt friendly, whereas this next step took me into a solid Victorian edifice with classes on three floors containing some of the toughest kids from a much larger catchment area than my previous school. Tony had been there before escaping to Beckenham Technical College and related stories of how hulking great delinquents were held down by two or three masters in order to be caned. In his time, Oakfield Road had contained Penge Central School for Boys and, by the time I got there, it had become Penge Secondary Modern. It was the old name-changing trick of trying to gloss over a place with a bad reputation.

There was one reassuring factor - Dennis Shipstone. His birthday was in June and he had transferred to Oakfield Road when the previous term started in September, and appeared to be in good health. Other lads from Anerley Junior days, including Len Quinnell, would also start with me at senior school but were not around on that cold January morning. It had snowed a few days previously and there was still enough frozen slush around to make missiles - in no way could they be considered snowballs - which became an additional hazard. Anerley school's playground had been extensive and at least a hundred yards from the public footpath; one came into it gradually. Oakfield's surrounding space was comparatively tiny, hemmed in and separated from the outside world by an iron- barred gate. On one side was the safety of the pavement; on the other a chaotic mixture of noise and an alarmingly active number of huge boys in long trousers. Lumps of ice filled the air. It was time to open the gate and grow up.

As with many other situations in life, outside appearances were worse than the inside reality. Oakfield's environment, being all-male, was certainly more boisterous and there were many 14-year-olds with deep voices making the most of their last playground days before being let loose into the working world. There was no school uniform; neatness was preferred, but there were a few outlandish touches, none more so than the lad who wore a large leather belt with a heavy metal buckle bearing the words "Gott Mitt Uns", allegedly looted from the body of a German pilot.

With several other lads, including Len Quinnell, I was ushered into Class 1A under the supervision of Mr Letch who, four years earlier, had been my brother Tony's teacher. Tommy Letch appeared to be in his late-somethings or earlyanythings; he was one of those time-warp teachers stuck in late middle age, always wearing the same dark salt-and-pepper suit with trousers which allowed plenty of room for those strange, hidden manipulations known among schoolboys as pocket billiards. He was a good teacher who encouraged my writing, tried to improve my arithmetic, and kept me, together with everyone else in the class, up to date with developments in the war.

Having been a soldier in the Middle East during the First World War, he was especially interested in battles being fought by the Eighth Army - the Desert Rats - along the coast of North Africa. "When I was in Palestine…" was one of Tommy's best-known opening phrases and had earned him the unofficial title, Lord Letch of Palestine. He was also Winston Churchill's greatest admirer and had, according to what he told the class, been a devotee long before the cigar-smoking statesman succeeded Neville Chamberlain as Prime Minister.

The fiercely-patriotic Tommy Letch was also inclined to war-inspired outbursts when dealing with some of his delinquent pupils. He would rush to where the lad was sitting, drag him to his feet and, with one hand on the rear part of the boy's collar, rock the poor kid violently with a backwards and forwards pumping motion while propelling him down the aisle between the desks. This would also be accompanied by Tommy's usual red-faced rant about "sailors risking their lives to bring you food." Obviously the Battle of the Atlantic was getting to him.

I only ever saw one lad who retaliated against these corrective methods. He was a ginger-haired little thug whose stick-out ears earned him the name Dumbo, although nobody ever had the nerve to call him that to his face. Dumbo flung himself at Tommy Letch with a shout about "always picking on me" and engaged him in a pushing match in which the boy was outweighed and sent back to his desk - but without being caned.

Other kids had different methods of scoring points off our teacher. It so happened that the door to our class was directly behind Tommy Letch as he stood facing the rows of desks, and he would be unaware that a lad who a few minutes earlier asked "to be excused" had returned and managed to enter silently. Carried away by the importance of whatever he was saying, Mr Letch would not know that a couple of feet behind him a boy was aping his every move and generally taking the mickey by pulling ghastly faces and making vigorous V-signs with both hands. These performances required co-operation by the rest of us who had to sit there with expressions of intense concentration while trying not to laugh. By some sixth sense, the perpetrator would suddenly turn away, rattle the door handle as if just closing it from the inside, and return to his desk while we all breathed a sigh of relief. I never saw anybody caught at this caper.

There were times when we left the classroom for periods of PT (physical training) with Mr Evans and singing with Mr Warren but - sheer delight - a whole morning each week was spent with Mr Love in the woodwork centre. In this separate single-storey building at the far end of the playground the usual classroom smell of chalk, sweat and unwashed boys was completely overcome by the meaningful tang of freshly cut and planed timber. Every boy was allocated a bench - and with it went a complete rack of tools, including chisels, saw, and wood plane, all of which were unbelievably sharp. Some of the boys I knew had fathers with sheds or workrooms containing similar tools; at home we had the bare basics of screwdriver, hammer and a small saw with a bent and wobbly blade. The woodwork centre was a revelation; its pine-smelling atmosphere and the sight of all that equipment aroused the urge to make things - and the kindly Mr Love was there to see that you went about it the right way, with planning and patience. Even today I still follow some of his basic rules.

As my first year in the senior school began, Tony was leaving the technical college. He had joined the Air Training Corps squadron in Beckenham - possibly through some association with his college friends - and continued as a member, but the schooling came to an end around Easter of 1942. There had been no leaving ceremony or even a final Friday homecoming at which he shook off the dust; he just stopped going to the college and started work somewhere in London. It was a firm with "Universal" in the title, producing artwork and lettering of some sort, and it was also the place where the middleaged Miss Hughes at number 15 Thicket Road (she of "Where are the wardens?" in Chapter 3) worked, although I have no idea whether she had anything to do with his getting the job. He was only there a short while and later began an apprenticeship with Samuel Stephens in News Buildings,

Belvedere Road, Upper Norwood, where the Streatham News Series of newspapers was produced.

This meant that Dad and Tony worked in the same building but not for the same company. To explain: Samuel Stephens was a large-scale printing firm producing everything from newspapers and magazines to leaflets, using letterpress and gravure processes; the Streatham News Series was part of a group called Provincial Newspapers and leased its editorial offices in News Buildings. It was a well-established and friendly relationship and Dad may well have helped Tony find his new situation; if so, it was the least he could do. Tony had never really completed his education at Beckenham Tech because the college required parents whose earnings were above a certain level to pay fees. Dad's salary took him into this category and, needless to say, he had defaulted.

It was something Tony never forgot despite going on to succeed in the business of photogravure and colour printing; it was also going to be an embarrassing factor for me a little later in 1942.

CHAPTER 6 - BUTTERFLIES AND OLD BIKES

While the succession of wartime events through 1942 and 1943 can be easily verified, matters concerning me, the family, and others around us in those two years are more difficult to date accurately. For example, we had an allotment on ground adjoining Anerley infants and junior schools, but for a short while there was also a second one much further away from Thicket Road, in a spot tucked away at the Sydenham end of Crystal Palace Parade. I only went to it a few times with Dad, but he must have started growing things there when Tony and I were away in Exeter. It was eventually given up and replaced by the Anerley allotment because it was close enough for Mum, Mrs Shipstone, Dennis, Beryl, and me to spend evenings there during 1942/3 and help grow a selection of vegetables. Dad used to put in a couple of hours on Sunday mornings before disappearing in the direction of a pub. Mum knew how to preserve some of the produce by salting - with which Margaret gave a hand - and pickling. Containers included large glass jars, probably from a friendly sweet shop owner, into which went shallots and red cabbage.

Writing this in 2014, I have just noticed an obituary in the "Daily Telegraph" about a wartime bomb disposal officer who had dealt with explosive Butterflies. This has prompted the memory of a visit to Oakfield School in 1942 by a woman from Civil Defence who warned us about these anti-personnel devices being dropped from German aircraft. The main part of a Butterfly Bomb was about the size of a can of baked beans to which a 12-inch metal strut had been attached half way along the barrel shape. When they were dropped, usually in batches, a spring release opened a pair of curved wings on each bomb, which slowed its descent and created a spinning motion that armed the TNT charge.

The Butterfly was not meant to explode on hitting the ground; it was designed to be found in the garden or on the street, caught up in trees or hedges - anywhere that an inquisitive person, particularly a child, would go to investigate and pick it up. Then it would explode, killing anyone within ten yards and causing serious injury up to 100 yards away. The Civil Defence woman had a defused Butterfly Bomb with her when she spoke at our school, and we took the message seriously. I don't know if any were dropped in our district, but they were used in other parts of the country and, despite warnings on posters, in the press and on the cinema screens, there were victims. (If you Google "Butterfly Bomb" you can see some of the publicity).

The combination of Tommy Letch's occasional meanderings, and the fact that I was getting a little bit older, certainly increased war-awareness. None of the kids around me were bothered when soap was rationed from February 1942, but we did wonder how in that month three huge German warships - the Scharnhorst, Gneisnau and Prinz Eugen - managed to get through the Straits of Dover without being sunk. We had to wait until May before the news got slightly better with a thousand-bomber raid by the RAF on Cologne, the father of one of our classmates, John Cullen, being among the aircrew.

It may interest younger readers of this to know that our schooling at that time, and indeed up to my leaving in 1945, involved no homework of any kind. We did not carry books to and from school; most lessons were taken by the form teacher (for us, Mr Letch, in 1A) while we sat at desks which contained, under the hinged worktop, all our exercise books plus the Bible, a dictionary, and a few other hardbacks. In the top right-hand corner of each desk was a china inkwell, replenished at times by the "ink monitor" - a kid who came around with a long-spouted and rather messy container. Pencils were used sparingly, most work was written in ink using pens with nibs which could produce decent letters and figures once they had been in use for a few days. Looked after properly, one nib could be made to last a couple of terms.

Among the hardbacks in my desk was "An English Heritage" containing sample chapters from a variety of books, with the aim of encouraging young readers to find out more by getting the complete volume from the public library. It certainly worked and led to my reading, for the first of many times, John Buchan's "The 39 Steps", and then "The White Company" by Arthur Conan Doyle and even - God bless it - "The Wind in the Willows" among many others. I had belonged to the public library, at that time in a building in Anerley Road next to the Betts Park entrance, since I was seven years old. It had an impressive junior section but made no effort to help younger readers find the books to suit their interests. Thanks to "An English Heritage" there were new authors to seek. Up to then, my favourite had been Richmal Crompton who produced the many adventures of William Brown and his Outlaw companions. I did realise after a while that William was being written to a format - each book had exactly the same number of pages - and that the illustrator had not quite mastered the art of drawing the lad's socks. But I still liked William, despite the shock of finding out from Dennis Shipstone that Richmal Crompton was a *woman*.

Back at school it was a bold move on somebody's part when, as part of a class reading exercise, we were issued with copies of "Biggles & Co" by W.E. Johns. An officially-sanctioned Biggles book! Under the direction of Tommy Letch, we went through the first chapter, but the following week he was absent and our class for this period was taken by the headmaster, Mr Margham. "I haven't read this book," he said. "What is it all about?" Of course we knew; we had talked about it among our friends and described the way in which Biggles, Algy, and Ginger were part of a company set up to transport gold bullion by air. But - and it is an important "but" - none of us had the confidence to describe this to the headmaster. After all those years of being told to sit down, shut up and listen, we could not face the simple task of standing up and making a vocal contribution of more than two or three words in class. To his credit, Mr Margham recognised the problem and set about restoring our lost voices and shattered confidence. For many of us it was a new chapter and one far more important than anything involving Biggles and his fellow fliers.

All the same, aircraft were an important part of our lives. They were the most visible part of the war and any noise in the sky prompted the question, “Is it one of ours?” I am not sure if the following piece of trivia is true now, but well into the latter part of the 20th century, Penguin’s biggest-selling paperback was “Aircraft Recognition”, produced in the early days of the war and a standard work for all military units as well as civilians. I know that our family had a copy. Most schoolboys could tell the difference between a Spitfire and a Hurricane by the shape of their wings as well as knowing that the German ME109 fighter had square wingtips.

I had been up close to a 109 when it was put on display in a car park (now the site of the Fairfield Hall) in Croydon. The fighter, with its pilot fatally wounded, had made a forced landing in a Kentish field and - apart from bent propellor blades and a few bullet holes - was intact. Later, in 1943, there was an American plane with square wingtips which initially caused dangerous confusion. That was the Mustang which I first saw while on the top deck of a trolleybus with Roy Caller, who lived next door to us in Thicket Road. The bus was approaching West Croydon when two low-flying aircraft, probably from the nearby airport, made a fast banking turn in front of us. “Mustangs!” we both shouted as they flashed past - and a woman behind us laughed. She wanted to know how we could tell, so we listed the vital points for her.

In 1942 I also had a close-up of a British Lancaster bomber parked in - of all places - Trafalgar Square, London. There was a National Savings Week called “Wings for Victory” in which every town and city set itself a target, usually with the stated aim of enough to buy a Spitfire or a couple of bombers. The bigger the community taking part, the more impressive-sounding was the target and - no surprises - the amount was always reached. I wondered at the time if these vast sums invested in National Savings actually stayed in National Savings or whether, like the small amounts I sometimes accrued, they were cashed in a few days later. However...back to the Lancaster bomber in Trafalgar Square.

At the start of “Wings for Victory Week”, Dad took us all on a No. 3 bus from Crystal Palace Parade into London. This was not his usual way of spending Sunday, so we made the most of it. As the bus approached Trafalgar Square from Whitehall I saw, parked on the area of the square nearest the National Gallery, a complete Lancaster in all its glory. It bore the initial H - for Harry - and the row of miniature bombs painted on the side of the aircraft just below the pilot’s cockpit showed how many raids it had made over Germany. Obviously the plane had been brought to London in pieces and then reassembled but it made an impressive sight. You could get close to it and, if you wished, buy National Savings stamps and stick them onto a couple of large-size bombs standing nearby. The promise was that these bombs, stamps and all, would be dropped on Germany.

While this seemed like a magnificent gesture it was not, I thought at the time, a very good investment. If you bought National Savings stamps and put them onto one of the cards they provided at the local post office you could, sooner or later (usually sooner in my case) get your money back. Clearly not everyone else was thinking along these lines because the bombs soon acquired a thick papery coating and a couple of weeks later they were dropped on a German target.

Penge made its own contribution to "Wings for Victory" by having a Saturday afternoon procession in which ranks of air raid wardens, the St John Ambulance Brigade, Home Guard and cadets representing the Army, Royal Navy and Royal Air Force marched through the High Street, past the Penge Empire. Shops had suitable RAF-themed displays and posters, while on the second floor of Rogers department store, an authentic rear-gun turret from a Wellington or Whitley bomber was featured. Even better, it was powered up and - if you were patient - you could have a turn at sitting in it while using simple controls to make the turret revolve left or right and alter the angle of the machine guns.

There was also an exhibition of air-war items at the old Melvin Hall in Melvin Road to which we were taken in school time and then, also in school time, had to write an essay. One of the exhibits was a parachute with which a wounded German pilot had escaped from his plane, and part of the harness was covered in bloodstains. I guessed that most of the lads would mention the blood, so instead I wrote something along the lines of the parachute being used and "...what was on the harness told its own grim story." Clever stuff. The idea was that the writer of the best in each class would receive 7s 6d in National Savings stamps - and there was also an exciting-looking book full of air-related stories, pictures and articles as a main prize for the best in the school. To my surprise I was best in the class and - an even bigger shock - received the book as well. On the way home I met Mum, who was with Daphne Crabbe, and told her the news about the essay. She was pleased but Daphne Crabbe asked, "Did your Dad write it for you?" I think she meant it as a joke, but Mum was not pleased.

I had to wait a couple of weeks for the savings stamps. One evening, with about a dozen other prizewinners, I went to an open-air presentation in Betts Park, in an area which had been fenced off as part of the Holidays at Home idea, (of which more in a moment). An amiable Kent county councillor named Russell Barnett handed out the pieces of paper and then we all stood together while Peter Eastment took a photograph which appeared in the "Penge and Anerley News." Earn money by writing...now there was an idea.

Holidays at Home came about because the government did not want large numbers of people travelling at any time, never mind the summer, because the railways and roads were a vital part of moving war materials. We had all grown used to seeing posters - yes, posters again - asking "Is Your Journey Really Necessary?" and in any case there was no point in going to the seaside because the beaches in the south and east were no-go areas covered in barbed wire and minefields. As Mr Letch constantly reminded us, "There is a huge German army less than 90 miles from London." Just as well that at least 22 miles of it was the English Channel.

In an effort to keep the population amused a little closer to home, many local authorities created fenced-off areas in their parks, containing the basics of a rostrum stage and all-weather seating. Throughout the weeks of summer there would be brass band concerts, guest appearances by entertainment groups and talent nights. I think the "Wings for Victory" presentation mentioned above took place during the interval of a concert.

Talent nights, which relied on a saucer-sized microphone and valve-driven public address system, could always produce a mixture of awfulness and genuine ability. The biggest surprise came on the evening the compere, Penge librarian H.G.T. Christopher, announced that there had been plans for ukulele-strumming George Formby to appear but that he was unable to make it. "However," he said, "we have Penge's own George Formby with us - Lenny Quinnell!" And to our astonishment, on came Len Quinnell, smiling and waving a ukulele banjo which had been decked out with red, white and blue ribbons. A quick adjustment of the microphone height, a nod to his cousin Peggy who took her place at the piano (where did that come from?) and Len was into a selection of Formby numbers, singing and strumming perfectly with all the technical wizardry, including split rolls. He walked off with the first prize.

After that, many of us scraped together the money to buy cheap second hand ukuleles plus the same pink-coloured instruction book which is still in use today. If the chords were simple enough, we could manage a small selection of tunes but Len was undoubtedly the best of our bunch. He had that enviable ability to play most instruments and read music - sharps, flats, keys major and minor. I have seen him play the one-string fiddle, piano accordion, trombone and tenor saxophone but not, as they say, all at the same time. With his brothers Les (double bass) and Charlie (drums) he later played tenor sax in a merry little group who called themselves The Celebrities and included my brother Tony on trumpet, plus school friend Pat Aylward on alto and clarinet, completed by a pianist called Brian Jones. At the time of writing Len is still, bless him, with us and the proud holder of a Musicians' Union gold card.

One other memory of Holidays at Home concerns Dulwich Park to which a bunch of mothers and kids set off one Sunday in the summer. There must have been eight or nine of us who caught a bus from Crystal Palace Parade, got off somewhere along Croxted Road and found our way into what was for us new territory. Dulwich Park was much bigger than Betts Park or Wells Park and in addition to a boating lake and putting green there was an area with seating and a stage. In mid-afternoon, a colourful troupe of entertainers arrived and announced themselves as being Russian, with the intention of playing "the music of the Cossacks." The women wore calf-length boots, short skirts with lots of petticoats and heavily-embroidered blouses; they had also gone to town with facial make-up and braids for their hair. The men kept pace with all this - wearing Cossack boots into which they had tucked the legs of their red trousers while their equally garish shirts had baggy sleeves. Despite the summer warmth, fur hats were worn.

The music came mainly from accordions and balalaikas (we wondered what Len Quinnell would have made of a triangular ukulele) and there were plenty of lively tunes plus some rather showy dancing. One of their number was the compere and, speaking English with a heavy accent, he carefully announced each item behind which, it appeared, there was always a tale of lost love, tragic death, crop failure, or starvation. The compere would emphasise the drama of all this by lifting his bushy eyebrows and saying "...but zee storee, aaahhh!" and drawing out the "aaahhh" until we all joined in. It was a great show, better than anything we had seen at Betts Park, and it cost us nothing.

The park was large, as I have said, and the gate by which we left was not the way we had gone in - result, confusion. Mum said we would have to go back, but I noticed something familiar about the lamp standards in a road ahead of us and insisted that we kept going. Nobody else believed me but I maintained that we would be able to catch a number 12 bus outside the Horniman Museum - and that is what happened. The bus took us to the bottom end of Thicket Road, completing a tour which had started at the other end of Thicket Road. The following year, when many of us had acquired bicycles, we would sometimes ride to Dulwich Park and enjoy the novelty of taking out a rowing boat for half an hour but we never again heard the "aaahhh!" of the Cossack compere.

There was another example of what I now call "the strip map mentality" when Dad took me to Selhurst Park one Sunday to see a wartime football match between Crystal Palace and Arsenal. The way to Selhurst Park from Thicket Road was simple enough: you caught a 654 trolleybus going away from Anerley Hill and in the direction of the Robin Hood crossroads where it turned right and continued on to South Norwood. Get off just past Norwood Junction and the football ground was (and still is) over on the right via Holmesdale Road. At the end of the match, however, Dad decided that the trolley buses would be overloaded and started to walk up Whitehorse Lane, on the northern side of the ground. I had never been that way before and felt we were walking in the wrong direction altogether - but you couldn't really say that to

Dad. It was a steep road and led into South Norwood Hill. We kept climbing and then we were in the familiar territory of Church Road, Upper Norwood. Even more familiar for Dad was The Alma pub on the corner of Belvedere Road where he said, “You know the rest of the way” - and disappeared inside. So I walked to the end of Church Road, down Anerley Hill and into Thicket Road, completing what was for me a strangely new circular tour. You did not, it seemed, always have to travel to and from places by the same route.

Incidentally, the match was the first time I had seen professional footballers in action, although many of them would also have been in one or other of the uniformed services. The Arsenal team contained both Compton brothers - Dennis and Leslie - as well as Ted Drake and two other names associated with the sea, Cook and Nelson. The result may have been a 3 - 3 draw but it must be in the book of Crystal Palace Football Club history. I wonder if my infants’ school headmistress, Mrs Cole, went to the game. By this time, Mrs Cole would have been responsible for the last of the Goldsmith trio, Margaret, who had started at the Anerley school and would follow the same route, via the “babies class” with Miss Lane, that I had taken.

Now that he was working, Tony could at last afford a slightly better bicycle than the one with which he had struggled for several months. His old machine was slightly bigger than a junior model and kept under cover in the communal hallway of number 19 where he would sometimes attempt to carry out simple repairs, usually in the evening. As the hallway was not blacked out he could not switch on the main light and had to rely on a torch held by me. I used to dread these occasions because the pattern was always the same; things would start well and then gradually deteriorate as he lost patience with the bike, the tools, and me, to say nothing of the torch, which got more feeble as the battery ran down. There was a crowning moment one dark evening when somebody turned up from the Beckenham squadron of the Air Training Corps to find out why Tony had not been attending its parades and evening instruction classes.

It was quite sad to hear my brother moaning about the difficulties of making enough time to get to and from Beckenham and having to make do "with this old grid of a bike" but to me the solution was simple enough: transfer from the Beckenham ATC to one much nearer - which is what he eventually did. He was much happier with the 1903 (Penge) Squadron and had various adventures, of which more later. Tony's slightly better second- hand bike - it had a three-speed gear, drop handlebars and slightly narrower tyres - meant that I inherited his "old grid" and was able to join Dennis Shipstone, who already had a machine, on ventures to places like Hayes Common, which meant riding down the notorious Corkscrew Hill just the other side of West Wickham. We could even go as far as Biggin Hill and stand on the road, watching fighters and transport aircraft coming and going.

But for a real day out there was nothing to beat the investment of sixpence in an all-day ticket which gave unlimited travel on trolleybuses and trams south of the Thames - but not ordinary buses. Described by my mother as "a jew-boy's excursion", the ticket meant being able to travel on a 654 trolleybus to West Croydon and then link up with the 630 service or, much better, hop on a tram and take the clattering, clanging route all the way to the Embankment in London, via Streatham and Brixton where you could get off, explore, and get on again. Two or three of us could go missing for most of the day, eventually returning at around teatime with enormous appetites and stories of where we had been. Yes, the war was still on, but London in 1942 and 1943 felt safe enough. I have since read "Up in the Clouds, Gentlemen Please", the autobiography of actor John Mills who worked in the capital throughout the war, describing London at that time as a place where "you could be killed at any time." His ghost-writer was suffering from an overactive imagination - unless he/she meant the risk of being run over by a bus or taxi.

Back at school there was a break in routine one day when, with several other boys from 1A at Oakfield, I was sent to Beckenham Technical College and sat a written exam which concentrated on practical rather than academic matters. I quite enjoyed it and a week or two later received a letter asking me to attend an interview. This was quite exciting; Tony had been to "the tech" and although I was not really interested in following his artistic line, I knew that there could be opportunities in other directions, including engineering and electronics.Yes, I was aware that my writing ability was above average but was still at an age when the world appeared to offer so much else. School at Oakfield offered a simple, even enjoyable, path from 1A to 2A and 3A before being let out at the age of 14 with nothing to show (we didn't have O Levels, A Levels or even Spirit Levels at that time) other than a reference from the headmaster. Nobody at home, especially my father, seemed terribly pleased about the forthcoming interview.

On the actual day he was in one of his black moods, surly and uncommunicative, but I was optimistic about my chances. The three men who questioned me seemed friendly enough until one of them asked, "Isn't your father the assistant editor of some newspapers?" I said that he was, the men looking at each other knowingly - and from there it all went downhill. It may well have been that I was a totally unsuitable candidate, but I have since wondered whether my father's financial record in paying - or not paying - for Tony's time at the technical college was one of the deciding factors. Whatever the reason, I would have to make the best of Oakfield.

Other people were doing better; Gwen Hughes, younger daughter of the family who lived at number 10, opposite us, had passed her 11-plus for the Beckenham High School, where she joined her sister Joyce. Their father and mother were likeable but with a hint of strangeness, which surfaced when the mother jumped out of a bathroom window and fell about 12 feet onto the steps at the front of the house. It was an early summer evening and our kitchen window, which looked over the road and down on the scene, was open. I heard a commotion, looked out and first of all saw Joyce who was crossing the road in our direction.

She looked up and called, "Is your mother in?" Mum was not in - and then I saw Mrs Hughes spreadeagled on the broad top step with blood coming from a gash to her head. A woman known among the Hughes family as Aunty Nelly, who either lived with them or near them, appeared from somewhere and cradled the injured mother while asking, "What have you done to yourself?" It seemed an odd question at the time, but it was later rumoured that Mrs Hughes had thought somebody was chasing her. Her injuries were not serious, but the whole incident seemed rather odd. Not long afterwards there was more strange behaviour - this time with Mr Hughes.

"Poppa" Hughes, as we called him, was a short and rather plump gentleman who worked somewhere in London and at the weekends played the organ at St John's Church, Auckland Road, Upper Norwood. Mr Hughes was always friendly and had a ready smile on his rather-too-red face, but it did seem out of the ordinary when I returned from school one lunchtime and heard him call to me as he leaned from one of the front windows of number 10. "Hello, Alan! How are you?" he shouted. He was wearing an overcoat and hat, his daughter Joyce was nearby looking worried, and without waiting for my reply he peered up Thicket Road in the direction of the railway bridge. "The signals have changed to red!" he reported and then, looking in the other direction at number 13, added, "Woburn House is wavering in the breeze."

As she prepared lunch, Mum explained that Mr Hughes was not very well and that if he spoke to you it was best to answer politely and keep moving. Over the next few days there were some harmless incidents including the old boy marching smartly up and down the street while barking military orders to himself. These exhibitions were usually heralded by a fortissimo performance of the Chopin Polonaise No.3 in A on his baby-grand piano. Mr Hughes continued to play the organ at St John's until one Sunday when he launched into a voluntary and refused to stop. The music continued until somebody had the idea of switching off the electric pump which provided wind power for the organ pipes. Although the instrument made a noise like a dying whale and lapsed into silence, the organist continued at the keyboard for half a minute or so before he realised that nothing was happening. According to some reports he then stood up on the organist's seat, waved his arms at the congregation and shouted, "One, two, three - go!"

Persuaded to return home from the church, our eccentric neighbour seemed all right for a few days but then overstepped the mark one evening when he started to get undressed in the middle of a busy Anerley Road. This traffic-stopping performance ended with Mr Hughes being restrained by several passers-by and then the police before an ambulance arrived and he was sympathetically removed. "Bye-bye, Poppa!" he called as the doors closed.

CHAPTER 7 - ECCENTRICS AND COMIC HEROES

The behaviour of Mr Hughes was one of the more extreme examples of eccentricity among adults seen by my friends and me. There were plenty of other harmless cases who would appear in our stretch of Thicket Road from time to time. One was a little man who always carried a Gladstone bag and walked with a peculiar rolling gait. His hat, worn with the front part of the brim upturned, was perched dead centre, but we were always fascinated by his kneebreeches - a great novelty to us - and the even more startling colours of the hoop-patterned stockings, which stretched from his boots over his calves. He had a clean-shaven face which shone with a just-scrubbed look and there was nothing at all frightening about his demeanour. On the handful of times we saw him he would speak to us in a piping voice, usually to warn that what we were doing was dangerous or, on one occasion, that the worn-out motor tyres being bowled to each other "might be needed by the coach for next week's Sunday school outing." He was harmless - but clearly not all there.

Also harmless was the little old gentleman who would give each of us small slips of paper on which he had pencilled indications of verses in the Bible which he felt we should study. He handed them out with a sincere "God bless you" and we would accept them with a smile and polite thanks, wait until the old boy had gone and then screw up the little bits of paper and flick them at each other. This venerable messenger was always accompanied by a slightly younger man who was tall, thin and dressed in the style of a City gent - morning coat with grey pin-striped trousers and spats. He wore a Homburg hat, had longish sidewhiskers and carried an umbrella with an ornate handle. I never heard him say anything to the old man or to the children who received the paper slips. There was a sequel a few years later when I had started work as a very junior reporter on the Penge and Anerley News and we received word that the old man had died. One of our senior reporters wrote the obituary.

The companion in the City gent outfit continued to be seen and appeared to become more and more eccentric as time went on. On the way through our street his walk would suddenly break into a high-stepping gallop which he kept up for two or three hundred yards as he stared into the distance. And then, panting and sweating, he resumed normal walking. Perhaps he had caught a glimpse of the paper slip distributor, beckoning from afar.

Others passing through our street included, for a time, old men who were billeted at Orchard Lodge, the group of buildings with a gated entrance on the west side of Anerley Road, not far from the infants and junior schools. We were never sure who they were or why they lived in a place none of us had ever really seen. These old boys had plenty of time to spare; they wandered the streets with eyes fixed on the pavements and gutters, looking for cigarette ends from which the tobacco could be rescued and combined with other "dog ends" to make their own roll-ups. Even if you had the money, cigarettes were hard to obtain - and these chaps did not appear to have money. One of them was known as "Billy Pudden" (don't ask me why) and he had occasionally amused local children by breaking into a dance. This was something I never saw although he always appeared to be fairly cheerful - apart from the time when I was with Margaret and she said, a little too loudly, "Look, there's Billy Pudden." He shot her a hurtful look and replied, "What's your name, then - Mary Jam Tart?" Obviously not in a dancing mood that day.

With so little traffic around at the time, our stretch of road was treated as a natural playground with few interruptions ("car coming!") to ball games and "kerb or wall" races. But there was also one person who could stop us in our tracks merely by walking from the Anerley Road end to the house - number 20 or 22 - where she lived. Although much of the foregoing has been about eccentrics, this lady was different only in her stunning good looks. Her name, as I later found out, was Madge Hunt and we usually saw her when she was returning, late in the day, from London where she modelled - even in wartime - the more fashionable items still available to patrons of whatever top store employed her. She never showed signs of having battled her way through the rush hour and always remained poised and elegant with perfect make-up and not one blonde hair out of place as she passed us, the scruffy youngsters who must have caused her some embarrassment by just staring in silence. It was, I have to stress, an admiring silence because we all thought she was absolutely beautiful.

I did manage to speak to the gorgeous lady one morning when delivering a message from my father - in his capacity as a warden - to Madge Hunt's diminutive father, also a warden and known as "Tiddler" Hunt. I went to the side door of the lower ground floor flat, was invited in and there she was, wearing slacks (then a novelty) and with not quite so much make-up, but still lovely and - a breathtaking moment - she actually spoke to me. I also met her husband, a rather nondescript-looking chap in RAF uniform, and her sister. Fast-forward twenty years and the sister was landlady of a pub near the back entrance to the Croydon Times works where my father was editor but I never found out what became of Madge Hunt. Wherever she went and whatever age she reached, I bet she was always a stunner.

So, where are we in the 1939 to 1945 time scale? Still somewhere in the region of 1942 and heading towards 1943, at a time when there was little serious German air activity in our part of the world - hence the trouble-free bus trips to London - and the war news was mainly about Russia, North Africa, and the Far East. I was still in the 1A class of Mr Letch whose patriotism and hero-worship of Winston Churchill had become an accepted part of our lives. There was the incident of the question-and-answer session when a boy asked, "Sir? If we win the war…" He got no further. "IF!?" thundered Tommy Letch. And again, "IF!?" adding "You mean

WHEN!" Yes, things were beginning to change in those far-off places but not for Penge schoolchildren. We learned to make the best of what we had.

Among the plus factors in our young lives at the time were comic papers like "The Dandy" and "The Beano". These were affected by the rationing of newsprint and appeared once a fortnight instead of weekly. This also applied to others such as "Film Fun" - of which more in a moment - and the string of story and serial-based publications. These included, "The Wizard", "Hotspur", "Adventure", "Rover" and "Champion" each of which, for the price of twopence, paraded its own regular collection of heroes and situations, some serious and a few light hearted. The golden rule in possessing one of these comics was: never throw it away. There were regular one-for-one swapping sessions among groups of four or five lads in which increasingly dog-eared comics changed grubby hands.

"The Dandy" and "The Beano" were comic-strip based papers, with most of the words appearing in balloons from the mouths of regular characters like Lord Snooty and his Pals ("Beano") or Korky the Cat ("Dandy"). There were many others - Pansy Potter the Strongman's Daughter and Julius Sneezer the Sneezing Caesar - as well as some whose job was to poke fun at our wartime enemies.

"The Beano" had Musso the Wop (He's a Bigga-da Flop) whose schemes always backfired while "The

Dandy" had an irascible character with a familiar-looking toothbrush moustache. He went under the name of Dick Tater and was constantly frustrated by failure. The term "brainwashing" had not appeared in those days but this was propaganda of a decidedly un-subtle kind. The outside pages, and some of the inside pages, were printed in colour - not garish but instantly recognisable.

By contrast, even in pre-war times, "Film Fun" was always black and white and continued the format of having Laurel and Hardy involved in an adventure which took them, frame by frame, from the front page over to the back cover. This impoverished pair - like their readers, always hungry - would occasionally be rewarded at the end of an episode by appearing in a final frame being wined and dined by somebody like the well-off Lottie Lotsadough at the Hotel de Posh where their table groaned with all sorts of unlikely goodies. Huge jellies and blancmanges would jostle for room among steaming joints of meat and - an absolute essential - a huge mound of sausage and mash. Glasses were being raised and everyone, including the scurrying waiters, was smiling.

The background detail in some of these picture-strip cartoon adventures was remarkable. A passing cat, while not essential to the actual storyline, would never be just a cat - it had to be carrying in its mouth the skeletal remains of a fish which still retained a tail at one end and a fed-up-looking head at the other. Scruffy dogs always appeared to be smiling and those with an upright stumpy tail did not seem to mind having a small union jack flag attached thereto. Cartoonland was a place where people left pies to cool on window sills and burglars wore masks and horizontally-striped jumpers while carrying bags marked “Swag”. In “Film Fun” it was also inhabited by passable representations of, among others, Old Mother Riley, and Joe E. Brown. Sydney Howard, I think, was replaced by Abbott and Costello, whose films were filling cinemas in the 1940s.

“Film Fun” was not all cartoons. Two of its pages were devoted to the written-down adventures of Inspector Stanley - the Man with a Thousand Secrets. The heading for these stories showed a thoughtful-looking chap with a pipe - a straight one, certainly not a curly Sherlock Holmes model. The narratives were fairly straightforward detective stuff during which there were usually moments when the inspector, while considering the facts, would pause to “flick an imaginary speck of dust from his trousers.” Obviously a fussy sort of bloke - and he always got his man.

Two other cartoon-based comics of the time were “The Knockout” and “Radio Fun”. The latter was a spin-off rival to the film-inspired publication and despite featuring representations of wireless favourites, including the ever-popular Arthur Askey, it never carried quite the same weight as the long-established “Beano” and “Dandy.” But for an absorbing hour or two there was nothing to beat the written adventures found in “The Wizard” and others of that group which, it has to be said, at least encouraged boys (and girls) to read. The stories themselves may not, by present standards, bear close examination but the actual spelling, punctuation, grammar, and sentence construction always set a good example. Each of these comics featured a mixture of four or five different tales every fortnight. Some were series, featuring regular characters in stand-alone stories, while others were in serial form with cliff-hanging episodes. Making sure that you read these in the right order was a minor complication when it came to one of the regular swapping sessions.

Wartime heroes found in these pages were, naturally, invincible - none more so that Rockfist Rogan RAF, who appeared in "The Champion". A boxer whose actual weight was never defined, he was also a fighter pilot for whom - typically - the second round of a thrilling fight for the squadron championship would be interrupted by a call to scramble and take off in his Spitfire with the rest of the chaps and meet incoming German aircraft. Rogan thought nothing of shooting down a couple of Messerschmitts, returning unscathed to his unit, climbing back into the ring and winning the boxing match while at the same time unmasking a German spy and solving the mystery of who stole the commanding officer's pushbike. Women were never part of his life.

This apparent celibacy also applied to one of the most memorable characters ever to thrill readers of "The Wizard." His name was Wilson - I can't remember his first name ever being mentioned - and he was an exceptional athlete whose long limbs were encased in a black leotard.

At least that's how he was shown, striding out with bare feet, in the regular title-piece of "The Truth About Wilson." The series, cleverly pitched as a biographical memoir told by a third person, was so convincing that people started writing to "The Wizard" to find out if Wilson had actually existed. He was, of course, fictitious - how else could he be stronger, run faster, jump further and higher and generally beat anyone else at launching a discus or javelin without staying out of the national news headlines?

Intriguingly, the recounted history of Wilson was set in the pre-war period and there were hints - later confirmed - of a self-imposed spartan upbringing somewhere in one of the wilder parts of the UK although his adventures took him much further afield. They would usually involve him in some puzzle or trial of strength before the actual event in which he was to take part. For instance, in one episode he was to take on a discus-throwing champion somewhere, possibly Greece, and needed to improve his technique. For this, he undertook a hazardous journey to study an ancient statue of a discus thrower perched somewhere on a remote island and this gave him the clue he needed. When the backlog of his many athletic conquests ran out and the story brought up to date, Wilson was shown to have an age of 60 or 70 although it didn't stop him joining the RAF and becoming a pilot.

Reading stories about flying was the nearest most youngsters at that time had ever come to being airborne.

My five-shilling flip at Croydon just before the war put me in a special category although there was a pre-war incident involving a lad who missed a day's schooling from his class at Anerley Junior. "Where were you yesterday?" asked the teacher. "Germany," replied the boy. This had to be a contender for the biggest lie of the year - until it was discovered that the pupil's elder brother worked in the freight section at Croydon Airport, had wangled a joy-ride on a round trip to Germany and took his little brother along as well. In the 1930s that was quite an eyebrow-raiser.

Belonging to the library enabled our imaginations to take to the skies via the books in which Biggles flew to all points of the compass but if you wanted real noise and spectacle it could be provided through the cinema with the Crown Film Unit's black and white "Target for Tonight" and "Coastal Command" or the more garish Technicolor of "Dive Bomber" with Errol Flynn and "Captains of the Clouds" featuring James Cagney. Even Abbott and Costello were there to provide comic relief in "Keep'Em Flying."

But whatever the films portrayed, going to the pictures was one of the ways of escaping into a warm, comfortable place where the huge moving images (kids usually sat down near the front) engulfed you in the plot, the action and the music. We had three cinemas in the immediate locality - the Rialto in Church Road, Upper Norwood and, in Penge itself, the Odeon and its near-neighbour, the King's Hall. I didn't go every week because the entertainment on offer was not always attractive enough and it seemed that whenever the current film in one picture house was a non-starter, the other two were also not worth the bother. On the other hand, all three would suddenly come up with must-see programmes in the same week - hence the simultaneous appearance of "Dive Bomber" at the Rialto, Walt Disney's "Dumbo" at the King's Hall and "Blood and Sand" with Tyrone Power at the Odeon. I had yet to learn that there were such people as film distributors in competition with each other.

The way I went to the cinema after school - that is, straight to the Odeon or King's Hall without going home first - was something regarded as quite normal. Mum, having provided the necessary shilling or less, would not expect me back for tea so that was all right. I would leave Oakfield School at the end of lessons and hurry through Hawthorn Grove, into Maple Road, down to the High Street and then along to, say, the King's Hall. Programmes consisted of a main feature and a supporting or "B" film interspersed with trailers for the following week's attractions, a newsreel, and an occasional Ministry of Information "short" dealing with a variety of subjects ranging from allotments and firebombs to cooking hints and tips on hygiene. There was even one about the proper way to wash your face.

The whole thing ran continuously, with a last complete programme starting around 7.15 or 7.30pm, so that getting there just before 5pm meant being able to see an early showing of the main feature. Then you saw the

"B" movie - which could be excellent - then trailers, newsreel and whatever, followed by (for you) a second showing of the big film. For a shilling or less you got about five hours of entertainment and a raging headache.

Not all films were about the war, thank heavens. Hollywood's flat-out schedules provided the public in America and the UK with a weekly diet of westerns, crime capers, comedies, musicals, and costume dramas which transported ration-hit audiences on this side of the Atlantic away from the drabness waiting beyond the cinema walls. One scene sticks in the memory: Fred MacMurray and Claudette Colbert, in a modern setting, were deep in conversation when a third character in the background produced a banana which he peeled and ate. Dialogue was drowned by groans from the cinema audience, who had not seen a banana, let alone tasted one, for two or three years.

Having been drawn into the war by the attack on Pearl Harbour in December 1941, America was also in need of some morale-boosting feature films and most of the earlier productions understandably cast Japanese as the bad guys. In flying sequences, a pilot from the empire of the rising sun usually died in closeup, amid the wreckage of a bullet-riddled cockpit canopy, head flopping forward while a trickle of blood spilled from the corner of his mouth. (Kids playing war games could imitate this effect by using a black cherry, provided they were in season).

So, pending any further developments, it was America versus the Japs while the rest of the English-speaking allies, plus Russia's forces, were taking care of the Germans. Winning UK audiences round to accepting the Soviets as recently acquired friends was helped by showing a full-length Russian film. All dubbed into English and called (I think) "Natasha", it featured the struggles of a village against Nazi invaders. There was also a short film called "Three in a Shellhole" in which two wounded soldiers, German and Russian, were joined in a battlefield crater by a female Russian nurse. She tended the wounds of both men but when her attention was distracted the German tried to shoot her, only to be killed by the other soldier. The film's message about rotten Nazis was quite clear.

Newsreels were an interesting mixture of non-war and war-related items in which the appearance of the King or Winston Churchill prompted applause, but the abiding memory is of the commentator's assuring, middle-of-the-road voice able to sound serious, triumphant, defiant or mocking, according to the accompanying footage. Carefully-chosen background music also helped to set the mood. Miserable-looking Italian troops surrendering in their hundreds in North Africa would be a typical target, accompanied by shots of burning enemy tanks and aircraft, swooping Spitfires or Hurricanes and cheery, thumbs-up smiles from our lads. Cue the voice with the sing-song stream of cliches. "...In the meantime, in the Western Desert, Mussolini's forces have been getting a taste of what it's like to be on the wrong end of a determined assault from the 8th Army. There's plenty more where that came from - and by the time our lads have finished, those spaghetti-eaters will wish they'd stayed at home!" (Increase the volume of marchy-marchy music).

Leaving the cinema at about 10pm was a gamble. To comply with blackout regulations, the exit consisted of two sets of doors separated by about 10ft of dimly-lit space. Entering this space was straightforward enough; pushing open the door that led to the outside was the surprising part. If the country was on double summer time - that is, clocks had been put forward two hours to help agricultural workers - then the street could still be in broad daylight. If the clocks had gone back to normal time, then you could stand at the top of the steps outside the King's Hall and stare into complete, baffling blackness.

Eyes would, eventually, adjust to the conditions but while that was happening it was necessary to stretch forward an exploratory foot, find the edge of the first step and then begin a cautious descent. There were three or four steps down to the pavement. Ears were strained to pick up the sound of what little darkened traffic may have been moving along the road; nearer, there were footsteps of other pedestrians and perhaps the glow of a cigarette or two. Getting home from the King's Hall meant turning left at the bottom of the steps, walking a few yards and getting ready for the first kerb - Kenilworth Road - again by foot-feel, crossing the road, judging the centre by its camber and then shuffling until you could feel the opposite kerb.

By this time, one's eyes would be on the way to adjusting; there might be a bit of moonlight to help and confidence would grow. The extent to which it was possible to see and sense one's way around under blackout conditions was remarkable - but that first post-cinema feeling always came as a shock.

I have already referred to the radio as another mainstay of entertainment and it did, indeed, continue to provide a steady stream of programmes from the Home and Forces stations of the BBC. The influence of teacher Tommy Letch, plus the fact that I was getting older, increased my interest in the news bulletins and the stream of place names from North Africa - notably El Alamein, followed by Mersa Matruh, Sidi Barrani, Tobruk and others too small to appear on our school atlas but big enough to be milestones as the 8th Army moved westward. Other place names from the Russian front, also small on the map, became huge tongue-twisters for BBC newsreaders like Alvar Liddel, Frank Phillips, Stuart Hibberd and the newly-introduced Wilfred Pickles - a man with an unmistakable Yorkshire accent. There was, for a few evenings in 1942, an additional interest when bulletins were interrupted by what became known as a "ghost voice" emanating from German-occupied Europe.

This is one of the episodes which has received little or no mention in the story of wartime radio although it caused quite a stir at the time. Bear in mind that news bulletins were read at a pedestrian pace of 100 to 120 words a minute, with plenty of pauses - something along the lines of: "RAF bombers were over Germany again last night……They attacked strategic targets in Cologne, Hanover and Essen…… Many large fires were started……Five of our aircraft are missing."

Imagine the reaction of listeners when, from their comfortable and dependable radio set, those pauses were suddenly filled with a German voice which claimed, "This is all lies!" and "They were all shot down!" These were not the drawling tones of Lord Haw-Haw but a different voice altogether - although it was something of a one-hit wonder, for various reasons. The shock use by the Germans of a "ghost voice" to cut in on news bulletins only worked properly on the first evening because newsreaders were unaware of what was happening. In addition, the interruptions were only on the long wave frequency while the medium wave was undisturbed. Apart from that, our enemies had completely failed to understand the British sense of humour. The voice which forced its way into our living rooms sounded like somebody mimicking a German trying to speak English; it was straight out of the music hall or even the radio's biggest comedy show, "Itma." Nobody in their right mind could take it seriously.

Of course there were plenty of high-ups in the BBC who did take it seriously. Bulletins had to be speeded up, and listeners were urged to listen to the news on the unaffected medium wave frequency rather than long wave where the voice lurked. Transmission power was stepped up and the voice, struggling to get a word into the accelerated flow of news, grew fainter. "Listeners may hear another voice trying to interrupt this bulletin," said a newsreader on the second or third night. "It *is* heard," insisted a faint and unconvincing whisper. That was the last time I heard it; our nine o'clock news lost its additional comedy element when the Germans gave up trying to be clever.

The radio was everybody's indispensable friend. It provided news, music, drama, a few panel shows and, above all, comedy. "Itma" - an acronym for "It's That Man Again" - was a showcase for the Liverpudlian Tommy Handley although "that man" when originally used by headline writers referred to Hitler. It was something of a coup for writer Ted Kavanagh to steal the title, attach it to Handley and create an astonishing range of other characters who popped in and out of each fast-moving wafer-thin half-hour plot. Whether he was the mayor of the fictitious Foaming-at-the-Mouth or, later, in charge of events on a strange island called Tomtopia, the show's anchor man was subject to the regular noise of a rattling door handle heralding the entrance of Mrs Mopp (Dorothy Summers), Ali Oop the postcard salesman (Horace Percival), or Colonel Chinstrap (Jack Train) among many others.

Each of these characters made a contribution to the plot but had - absolutely had - to deliver their own catchphrase before departing to a round of applause from the studio audience. Mrs Mopp was the cleaner (charlady) who asked, "Can I do yer now, sir?" while Ali Oop's offers of dubious merchandise were always turned down and he left with the words, “I go - I come back” The toping Colonel Chinstrap conveniently misheard everything as an offer of a drink (Handley: “My patience is wearing thin.” Chinstrap: “Sherry and gin? Wonderful idea - I don’t mind if I do.”). There were, over the years, dozens of different catchphrases and these, as I have said before, provided a link which could produce smiles from strangers.

I also became a regular listener to “Saturday Night Theatre” because my mother, at the end of a ration-juggling week, used to join my father for an evening drink at the CPH (Crystal Palace Hotel), the Alma in Church Road or perhaps the nearby Thicket Hotel. Tony, well into his teens, would be out somewhere and this left me to sister-sit with Margaret, who usually went to bed at about eight o’clock. “Saturday Night Theatre” began at 9.20pm on the Home Service and lasted until 10.45. The familiar voices of Laidman Browne, Belle Chrystal, Grizelda Hervey and others acted out stories old (“Young Woodley”, I remember, and “An Inspector Calls”) as well as new. The only trouble was that my parents, sometimes with overly-cheerful friends in tow, would occasionally return at about 10.30 and drown the final part of the radio drama with their chatter.

Dad was getting very busy at about this time. His day job was, as I have said elsewhere, assistant editor of the Streatham News Series of nine local weekly papers, which had offices in News Buildings, Belvedere Road, in

Upper Norwood. News Buildings also housed the extensive works of Samuel Stephens Ltd which, in addition to printing the newspapers, turned out other publications. Some of these were produced using the high-quality photogravure process about which my brother Tony was learning as an apprentice. So, he was also working at News Buildings - and a few years later I would be there as well.

Bear with me while I go into further explanations. If you go to the top of Anerley Hill you are on the southern edge of the London basin. Look back to the south-east and you can see across a large part of Kent and Surrey; cross the road and walk a few yards along Westow Hill, then look north in the gaps created by Jasper Road or Woodland Road and you can see across London, over the dome of St Paul's and, depending on conditions, well beyond. So, News Buildings, sharing this height, was an ideal spot when the Daily Mirror Group established a listening post for monitoring news broadcasts and other programmes from occupied Europe.

The Mirror rented a large room and established seven or eight powerful receivers, plus a teleprinter link to their offices in Fleet Street. Dad managed to join the part of the team which concentrated on German output and, as these additional working shifts began in the evening, he could walk from his daytime office to the radio room in less than a couple of minutes. The only problem was that if he took sandwiches with him when he left home in the morning, they would be pretty well dried up by the time evening came. Thus began the routine of my taking Dad his sandwiches which had been made in the late afternoon.

I would get there at six or just after, when the newspaper offices had shut for the day, and on the first couple of occasions had trouble getting past the ancient Irishman who guarded the main doors of the printing works. These were closed but they contained a smaller door at which the old boy would appear. He eventually let me in and insisted on my being escorted through the works and upstairs to the radio room where, in a pall of cigarette smoke, I could make out my father and several other people. Sandwiches delivered, I left and made my way home again.

As the routine developed, the guardian would simply wave me through and I found my own way, taking my time and at first discovering, and then savouring the atmosphere of a printing works. It was a mixture of dust and freshly-cut paper overlaid by the oily tang of printing ink; I picked my way between stacks of publications, many of them already bundled and labelled, and on certain nights there would be the sound of machinery, on Thursdays the roar of the rotary press producing the following day's "Clapham Observer", "Streatham News" or "Mitcham News and Mercury" or sometimes the steady thud-thud thud of a smaller press; and occasionally both. Men in brown overalls or dark blue boiler suits gave me only a passing glance.

My father once asked a young compositor to give me a tour and I was shown places well beyond my usual route through the works. There was a battery of Linotype machines setting stories into galleys of lead-based "slugs", the foundry in which curved metal plates were produced for locking onto the huge rotary press and, apart from the impressively-sized machinery, there were benches and shelves containing tools for chopping and scraping the metal type, plus a hand-operated press for proofs which went to the reading room to be checked.

My guide demonstrated the small press by using a rubber roller to put ink on an item he had taken from a nearby shelf. He covered it with a piece of paper, then produced the finished item - which in this case illustrated the quirky sense of humour for which the printing industry is notorious. Another explanation: a packet of twenty cigarettes at that time came in a light cardboard container on which was printed the brand name - Players or Churchmans, for example. Part of this container could be unstuck and reversed, leaving plain white card. What had been produced on the small press was an alternative brand name, to be printed on a reconstituted packet. Together with a suitable equine illustration, the bold type read "Genuine Horse Shit Cigarettes" - a guaranteed conversation stopper when it was produced in a fuggy pub.

At the time, the serious output from Belvedere Road also included "True Story" and "True Romance" magazines, printed by the gravure process, as were batches of leaflets to be dropped by the RAF on enemy and occupied territories. There was nothing romantic about some of the illustrations on these. Much more cheerful was the black and white magazine "Blighty", produced in runs of several thousand for free distribution to HM forces. Its pages of cartoons by artists including Arthur Ferrier and Tom Cotterell also contained short stories and general morale-boosting cheer for serving men and women in every theatre of war. Tony used to bring copies home - and a fair number must have also leaked into the locality because when a newsreel at the Rialto cinema included a brief close-up of an 8th Army soldier reading "Blighty", there was a perceptible "Aah!" from the audience.

One other free publication, worth noting from a historical point of view, was "Good Morning!" - a Daily Mirror-inspired tabloid produced at News Buildings exclusively for sailors serving on submarines. This had the appearance of a newspaper without actually being one because it had been printed and delivered weeks ahead of the time it would be read. Nevertheless, its writing and presentation of stories gave it the appearance of being hot off the press. "Good Morning!" also carried the Mirror's bunch of serialised strip cartoons, chief of which - and with the emphasis on strip - was Jane, the glamorous and somewhat ditzy young lady whose daily adventures often involved loss of essential clothing. The quartermaster on each submarine kept "Good Morning!" under lock and key and was on trust to distribute identical batches of a dozen or perhaps twenty - depending on crew numbers - at the beginning of each day. The proper sequence had to be observed and, no matter what predicaments Jane or any of the others were getting themselves into, the crew had to wait until the following day to see what happened.

After the war, the Mirror told the story of one real-life incident in which a submarine was trapped on the ocean floor with no apparent hope of escape. To help placate the crew, the quartermaster actually relented and gave out the future copies of "Good Morning!" so that the lads could at least see what happened to their favourite cartoon characters. The fact that the story could be told also meant that the submariners did, after all, survive.

Like most large factories, Samuel Stephens Ltd had to guard against incendiary bombs dropped from German aircraft. The company was required to post a firewatch rota of its own personnel who, when rostered, stayed on the premises, sleeping on camp beds and then taking up station on the flat roof when air raid sirens sounded. Everyone had to take their turn, including my brother Tony and another young man from his department who was deaf and dumb and known in those non-PC days as Dumbo. Under the letter of the law he had to be a firewatcher even though - and this was pointed out in certain quarters - he needed to be told in sign language when it was time to go up on the roof, was unable to hear bombs of any kind and, if he did spot a firebomb, was also unable to raise the alarm by shouting. Dumbo may have had his problems, but so did the authorities; they must have been blind.

Getting back to the subject of the Mirror's wireless receiving station, my sandwich-delivering visits to the room were not always hasty. On one occasion, when Dennis Shipstone was with me, we were both invited to sit down at radios that were not being used, put on headphones and explore the different frequencies. The music was fine but the multiplicity of languages other than English was completely baffling although, when English was heard, it was usually from an unfamiliar voice with a foreign accent.

In the meantime, other radio receivers were being more usefully employed by the Mirror team which included "Bunny" Hutter (or Hutte), who had served in the German army during the First World War, and a Dr Woolf. There were some I did not meet who listened to output from Hungarian and Russian stations.

On another occasion I sat and watched my father as he monitored a German news broadcast and took a verbatim shorthand note in English. At the end of the bulletin he picked up his notes, walked over to the teleprinter and started typing his report to the Mirror offices: "German radio last night claimed that…" The text which followed contained full "quotes" from the broadcast which he had noted in the squiggles and dots which I later learned about from my first Pitman's primer. Dad had filed his news story in a manner and speed which, at the time, I failed to appreciate. It had involved instantaneous mental translation of the German into English and then into shorthand, then reading back his notes and selecting the newsworthy parts while writing the story on the unfamiliar three-bank keyboard of a teleprinter. All done and dusted in a matter of minutes.

One of his contributions was a poem the Germans broadcast as the fortunes of war turned against them. It was called "Germany Will Bloom Again" - and while it called for a little extra skill in translation the result made an eyecatching item in the following day's paper.

Not far from News Buildings was another monitoring station, run by a news agency. The method there was to have one person who took a note in German shorthand and afterwards translated it into English. The text would then be passed to a journalist who used the material to write a story - the whole process taking well over an hour. Throughout the war, the agency never managed to sell one German-based story to the Mirror.

CHAPTER 8 - WHO WENT WHERE

Whereabouts are we in the time and space that I am recalling? End of 1942 and into 1943, possibly. One thing was certain: we were winning the war and occasional treats came into shops as the Battle of the Atlantic swung in our favour and fewer ships were sunk. We still spent evenings on the allotment, joined at times by the neighbouring Mrs Shipstone with Dennis and Beryl. Even the rather substantial Daphne Crabbe helped out as we tended our rows of vegetables and trudged backwards and forwards to the point where watering cans could be filled. I was not there on the occasion Mum prodded our compost heap and disturbed a wasps' nest - with alarming and painful results. From one of his many contacts, my father obtained a small white cube of something which had to be kept carefully wrapped until it was inserted into the nest entrance. There were mutterings about it being "enough to wipe out half of Penge", so I kept well away. The wasps gave no more trouble.

Marginally less lethal was the other white crystalline stuff which my father intended to spread on the allotment to help things grow. It was in a medium sized paper bag which appeared in our kitchen and went no further. Probably because it was autumn or winter, there were no visits to the allotment and the bag was placed out of the way in a deep drawer which also contained a tin of shoe polish, brushes and other household bits and pieces, including our one and only screwdriver. The paper bag gradually disintegrated and these white crystals became mixed up with the other contents of the drawer - all a bit messy, until the Sunday morning when my mother decided that it was time for a clear-up. Normal contents of the drawer were taken out, allowing her to tip the crystals into a metal bucket (no plastic in those days) to be taken downstairs and emptied into our dustbin. Before that, however, still-warm ashes of the previous night's kitchen fire were added.

None of us had realised that the white crystals were sodium nitrate - and there was enough heat in the ashes to set off an involuntary firework display as the kitchen filled with a choking smoke. My father, listening to the radio in the adjoining lounge (or "front room" as we called it) was unaware of Mum's disastrous clearing-up caper until her shouts disturbed him and he discovered a blazing bucket on the mat in front of the kitchen fireplace. There was, fortunately, a bucket of sand in a corner just outside the door of the flat. Placed there in 1939 in case of incendiaries being dropped by the Luftwaffe, it finally came into use as Dad emptied most of its contents onto our own home-made firebomb. The smoke cleared, the bucket cooled down - and another Goldsmith story was born.

Dad was surprisingly good-humoured about what could have been a disaster - but he had, after all, been the one who brought the sodium nitrate into the flat and left it around.

Our allotment, as I have probably explained, was on land backing onto the north side of Anerley school by the Town Hall. On one side was the wall dividing us from the school playground, on the other - separated by a wire mesh fence - was the land belonging to Orchard Lodge. This establishment, with a gated entrance onto Anerley Road, was always a mystery. The old, fag-end- seeking men from the early part of the war seemed to disappear as we moved further into the 1940s. Instead, there were uniformed figures - a mixture of regular soldiers and members of the Home Guard - and I heard for the first time the sing-song, repetitious voices of military instructors. Beyond the fence were buildings and glimpses of metal structures not unlike the Bofors and other guns any keen-eyed youngster would recognise from pictures in newspapers, or from feature films in which troops or sailors fired at German aircraft. One big difference, however: these weapons - if they were weapons - did not appear to have barrels. We would find out more within a few weeks.

Meanwhile, life in our short stretch of Thicket Road was tolerable, even comfortable, as broken windows and other war damage was repaired. True, the clear glass in our kitchen window had been replaced with a distorting pane of something more usually associated with a bathroom but at least we had daylight if not a view of events in the street.

Now for an attempt to recall as many as possible of the families who were part of our lives at that time, starting on "our" side of the road - the odd numbers (no pun intended) - with number 19 and its four flats. Bear in mind that the grand houses in Thicket Road were built as single households with accommodation on five levels for middle-class families employing servants. At some time the owners had decided to split them into flats, aided by a limited amount of ingenuity and an apparently endless supply of tongue-and-groove boarding. Self-containment was achieved for most but not all future residents.

We - Dad, Mum, Tony, Margaret and I - were in the uppermost part of the house; the flat below us was unoccupied for some time but would soon be taken over by Nurse Martin, of whom much more later. The hall flat, vacated early in the war by the childless Mr and Mrs Brown, had a succession of temporary tenants including a bombed-out family from the Parish Lane area; then a couple rumoured to have criminal connections; followed by an RAF bomber pilot, his wife and baby. The Battens - Bert, his wife and daughter Win, followed later. In the basement we had the seemingly eternal Blakes who produced two daughters during their time in Thicket Road and insisted that they occupied "the garden flat." This did not impress Mum who gave short shrift to any inquiries. "Blake? In the basement."

Next to us, at number 21, the middle flat was occupied by the elderly Mundells - Queenie and her long-suffering husband Alfred. Queenie was a regular customer at the Thicket Hotel, our nearest pub a few yards up Anerley Road on the corner of Lullington Road. I don't know what she drank, but it had a dreadful effect on her husband, who bore her shrill insults with dignity. In the hall flat lived Roy Caller, a year or so younger than I, whose parents were on the verge of splitting up. His diminutive mother took great care of her appearance, worked in London, and spent a lot of time among the increasing number of Canadian troops in the capital. A tryst with one of them in a surface air raid shelter helped put an end to her marriage. Roy's grandmother also lived in the flat until she dropped dead one afternoon. In the basement at 21 was the Hone family - husband, wife, a couple of scruffy girls, joined later by a baby brother or sister. There was also a foul-mouthed old biddy known as Granny Sullivan. She was constantly threatening trouble - "There'll be some shit flying in a minute," was her usual cry.

In one house further down, number 23, were Mr and Mrs Sims, their daughter Daphne and small son Mickey. The lad always seemed to be crying that "I've got no one to play with" - the word "pla-aa-ay" being dragged to three times its normal length as he broke into tears. Mr Sims was not old but did not appear to be in good health. He worked among the squads who went round demolishing the dangerous remains of bombed buildings and was also a member of the Home Guard but died of cancer in 1943 or 44. Mrs Sims was not a likeable character, although she seemed to get along with neighbouring women. Her daughter acquired a kitten and called it Benjy, unaware that it was female until a litter of kittens appeared. Mrs Sims put up with this growing family of moggies until she decided that it was time to take them all, including Benjy, down to the RSPCA in Penge. It was late afternoon when she set off with a wicker basket but half way there the air raid sirens sounded and people began running for shelter. Mrs Sims opened the basket and while its feline contents fled in all directions, she headed home. Working in one of the canteens in London for American servicemen, her tasks included operating the waffle machine - an apparent necessity for fighting men who required a constant supply of hot wafer-like material drenched in syrup. Mrs Sims never really understood the differences between her everyday use of English and that of her US customers. “The other day I called one of them a bastard and he was most upset,” she told my mother.

Occupants of number 25 were never familiar to me but I do recall the rather pretty wife of a serviceman. She may have been living there with her in-laws. Her husband was taken prisoner in the Far East and managed to survive, although when I saw him shortly after the war ended he was walking in a trance-like state, with his family each side in close support.

Now a step back up the road, past 19 to number 17, where on the first floor (or hall flat) were Mr and Mrs Stubbs, the latter christened “Nosey” Stubbs because she never strayed far from the window facing the street. Any misbehaviour by youngsters - like me climbing on the dividing brick wall - brought a series of sharp raps on the glass. In the basement were the childless Mr and Mrs Tuppen who had moved there after a short time in the hall flat of number 19. It must have been in 1943 that I told Mr Tuppen about my school’s toy-making enterprise in raising funds for the RAF. He suggested that I could help him make a wooden toy locomotive - and that is what we did in a series of weekly meetings in the small room, virtually a large cupboard, that he had converted into a workshop. Mr Tuppen could work marvels with wood and it took only a month or so to produce a substantial toy with a brilliant red-painted finish. Put up as a raffle prize at school, it raised a generous sum.

Moving along to number 15, we meet again with Miss Hughes, the rather panicstricken lady from earlier in this narrative - the one who, on the night our windows were shattered, had been shouting, "Where are the wardens?" To be fair, on that occasion she was worried about the effect on her 90-odd year-old mother who made occasional appearances in the front garden where she sat and admired the flowers grown by her daughter. Miss Hughes worked in London, doing something artistic, and spent a lot of her spare time nurturing what was undoubtedly the best-looking front garden in our part of the road. She did not seem to like children; any of us trying to look through the hedge while she was watering the flower beds was liable to get an "accidental" drenching.

Hedges, incidentally, formed the main border between front gardens and the footpath ever since the morning when a lorry appeared and men with sledgehammers removed the wrought iron railings, supposedly to melt down and built tanks and guns. Like an earlier campaign to collect scrap aluminium for aircraft, it was later proved to have been of little practical use.

Back to Miss Hughes for the moment. Her mother died before the war ended and suddenly Miss Hughes became Mrs Bishop, with a husband called Alfred. It was a surprise for everyone including Mrs Shipstone, in the basement at number 13, who used to earn a few shillings working as a "daily" (cleaner) for her neighbour. Before the marriage there was an incident which resulted in Mrs Shipstone (or "Shippy" as many of us knew her) leaving Miss Hughes a note saying that she no longer wanted to work for her. It was a snowy winter night when an overwrought Miss Hughes stomped round to number 13 and banged on Shippy's door. Words were exchanged and it all became rather undignified, especially when Miss Hughes slipped over and rolled around, trying to get up. Shippy then had the novel experience of being harangued by an hysterical snowman. Good sense eventually prevailed - but it must have been hilarious.

Number 13's basement flat - called 13A for address purposes - was the home of Mrs Shipstone, her son Dennis, and daughter Beryl, but I can remember a fourth person living there when I first knew Dennis back in 1935. It was an old man who sat and gave me a suspicious stare, seeming to resent my being there for tea at the invitation of Dennis. It was, I think, Mrs Shipstone's father, and I only saw him once because he died. The flat, as I have explained elsewhere, was also a haven for our whole family on blitz nights and also gave shelter to many others in the last year of the war.

Again, in an earlier part of this story I have referred to the Frost family from the top flat, with the breadwinner who worked as a projectionist at the King's Hall cinema in Penge and described the details of films in graphic terms of "heroes" and "shitbags." The house was owned by the Howard family, who occasionally used the middle two floors, although little was seen of them, and Mrs Shipstone would be visited at times by an affable woman of the no-nonsense "Right-ho, troops" kind. At least Shippy saw her landlord; in all the years we lived at number 19 I never knew who owned the place - we just paid our twelve shillings and sixpence a week at the tiny office of Noyes and Hows, the estate agent at the far end of the railway bridge near the Town Hall.

Move next door to number 11 and there lived, for a short while, a lad called Dennis Freeman who was never really a member of the long-standing gang of kids and moved to Eastbourne with his family when they took over The Beach Hotel, near the lifeboat station at the east end of the town. At number 9 there were real youngsters, Geraldine and Ian, the pre-school children of Mrs Pat Jacobs, separated from her husband who was, in any case, in the forces. The children attended a day nursery in Anerley Road, quite a long way down past the library, while their mother worked in London.

The youngsters had to be picked up each weekday evening by the ever-busy Mrs Shipstone and taken to their flat at number 9 where, with their carer, they waited for Mrs Jacobs to return. Ian was the younger of the two while

Geraldine was about three and possessed a deep, mournful voice in which she expressed equally gloomy thoughts. "All cold, all dark," she would moan on returning to an unlit and unheated home. On another occasion at Knight's the grocery shop she saw one of the senior male assistants open a trap door and descend into the cellar. When he had disappeared completely, her little gloom-ridden voice announced, "Poor uncle! Fall-ee down big 'ole."

Geraldine's mother had, before her marriage, worked at the film studios where they produced the comedies starring George Formby. She herself was good at producing children - the third, a girl, arrived while she lived in Thicket Road but Mrs Jacobs remained unattached - unless you count the occasional American serviceman. These were, of course, strange times for everybody.

Beyond number 9 - at 7 or 5, I am not sure - were the Everitts whose family head owned and ran the business, on the upper part of Anerley Road - same side as the greengrocer (Burley's) - of taking photographic portraits. The shop window - when it wasn't shattered by bomb blast - showed high-class work ranging from large groups, taken with a special panoramic camera, to well-posed individuals. Along the way, Mr Everitt had also picked up the pre-war business of taking individual pictures to be sold as postcards to fans of speedway riders in the Crystal Palace team. I never met Mr Everitt senior, who died early in the 1940s, but knew his son a few years later. His widowed mother, who never mixed with the women in the other part of Thicket Road, once caused a minor stir by taking a walk in the sunshine. As she paraded past in suitable hat, summery dress and holding up a miniscule parasol, one observer (Mrs Hone, I believe) observed, “Cor, look at ‘er! Old titti-fer-lah.” High fashion - of whatever era - was never appreciated in our part of SE20.

I cannot be as detailed about the people on the other side of the road - the even numbers - but some of them were interesting. At number 2 was a family headed by the uncle of Daphne Crabbe, who called him “Nunc.” Daphne also lived there, having lost her immediate family earlier in the war when a bomb fell in Anerley Park and she herself had a narrow escape. “Nunc” was a sergeant in the Home Guard and will be mentioned again later. Number 6 had a number of individual tenants - Irish-sounding nurses who worked at a house further down Thicket Road - beyond the railway bridge - where some sort of care home had been established. In the basement at number 6 were the Librettos, including a son Dennis and daughter June.

Next door at number 8, tenants in the basement came and went but the firstfloor hall flat was the long-established home of the Whites. Mr White was well known as a milkman for United Dairies and his years of service included a prewar accident in which his foot slipped from a metal step leading up to the seat from which he controlled his horse-drawn milk float. The horse kept going and the cart ran over Mr White’s leg, as a result of which he walked with a limp. Every lunchtime the milk float was parked outside number 8 and the horse was generally patient in waiting for its driver to return. Occasionally it would decide to supplement the contents of its nosebag by eating a nearby hedge and there was a time, just after the war, when it decided to have a lie-down - an occasion when my father lent a hand in dissuading the horse and showed a skill which surprised me and several other people. Long-ago experience as a farmer's boy was not wasted.

As for Mrs White, she was a very quiet person but her younger daughter Pamela more than made up for that once a week. Anybody hearing multi-decibel shrieks would be excused for thinking that murder was taking place; in fact, Pamela was having her substantial mop of blonde hair washed. You could hear her from the kitchen of our flat on the other side of the road. The White's eldest was a son, although we never saw much of him, and there was another daughter, older and thankfully a lot quieter than Pam.

In the upper part of number 8 lived Ian Robinson, a classmate with me at Oakfield, whose younger brother was named Stuart Holmes. Ian's mother had divorced and was married to Joe Holmes. Ian and I were great friends for two or three years, including the time we were both evacuated to Exeter and I managed to contact him there. Back in Anerley we walked to Oakfield School together and, during a period when each of us paid five pence a day for school dinners, sat together and ate some rather peculiar meals. There was also time during these extended lunch breaks to go around exploring bombed-out buildings. Nearer home, we also tried to make things out of debris from damaged houses, dumped by the roadside to await collection. In among the rubble one could find interesting items including, on one occasion, a glass-fronted shallow box which contained a series of electro-magnets.

It was an indicator, probably placed on the wall somewhere in the servants' quarters where, with an electric-powered bell, it would have shown from which room in the upper part of the house one of the downstairs menials would have been summoned. Ian and I managed to separate the magnets and tried to make some sort of electric motor, but failed. Also unsuccessful were our attempts to make an elementary radio receiver - but it was fun trying.

Opposite our house was number 10 where the upper rooms were taken by the Hughes family. I have mentioned the breakdown of "Poppa" Hughes and other matters in an earlier chapter but have to add that I was always very fond of Gwen, the younger daughter, who was always organising things for other children - usually younger members of the Hone and Sims families - in the vicinity. These included a lending library in one of number 10's attic rooms - it came to a premature end when a book donor was taken ill with scarlet fever - and a pets' cemetery. The latter feature began when Gwen's rabbit, named Peter, died and was buried at the far end of her garden. It was soon joined by a variety of creatures, found by Gwen and her devoted group, then carried off to be buried with due ceremony in which the Lord's prayer and National Anthem were an essential part. Sneaking into the garden one afternoon I came across an inscription: "Here lies the wireworm which died in great pain…" Gwen's funeral gang must have been getting desperate.

Also in number 10 were Mr and Mrs Rideout on the hall floor and, in the basement, Mr Tom Arnold and his wife - soon to be hit by tragedy.

Bear with me while I complete the Thicket Road cast by going to number 12, where the tenants included Mrs Stebbings and a son of seven or eight named Kenneth. He wasn't the brightest of kids but was it really necessary for some of his schoolmates to stamp on his toes when they knew he had chilblains? His father returned from army service before the war ended and proved to be an interesting character.

At number 14 were the Staceys - father, mother and young daughter, with another arrival late in the war. Also there was Nurse Martin, district midwife, who moved into the flat below us in number 19 during 1943. More of her later.

Memory banks have drawn a blank as far as number 16 is concerned but number 18 housed the Mantles and the Davis family who had an enterprising son named Terry. His worldly possessions included a selection of goods discarded by people vacating their homes - various non-working watches, books and at least one portable gramophone. “Where did you get that, Terry?” he would be asked. The answer was always the same: “Empty ‘ouse.” He never disclosed his methods of entry.

We were an interesting bunch in that short stretch of Thicket Road between Anerley Road and the corner of Lullington Road as we moved into 1943, riding out the war and blissfully unaware of what was to come.

CHAPTER 9 - THREE 109S AND A ROCKET

By the start of 1943, every news bulletin on the BBC Home service either started with or contained news of the previous night's RAF bombing of Germany; then bombers from the American forces stationed in England began their daylight raids. Hitler's forces were losing ground in Russia and the Middle East - but at the time of our key victory at El Alamein, Winston Churchill had warned that it was "not the end, or the beginning of the end, but perhaps the end of the beginning." There was plenty more to come on the home front, as I found out just after midday on Wednesday, January 20th.

School dinners had lost what little charm they had and I was going home for the lunch break, a few minutes later than the main rush of boys, because I wanted to sneak home my bottle of school milk - a third of a pint - and use it to make junket. This treat, a forerunner of the now widely-produced yoghurt, could be made by warming a small amount of milk in a saucepan, adding a flavoured tablet which contained rennet, and then pouring it all into a glass. Left to set, it became a teatime treat.

As I crossed the school playground towards the Oakfield Road gate I heard rapid deep-toned gunfire, loud enough to make me think that something was being test-fired in the nearby grounds of the Crystal Palace. Gunfire had never been heard from that direction before - but what else could it be? No air raid warning had sounded. I stepped into Oakfield Road, then saw an aircraft approaching from the Penge end of the road, flying really low - less than 100ft - and banking away to its left to reveal black crosses and the squared-off wingtips of a Messerschmitt 109. I crouched by the school wall as the roar of the engine faded, only to be followed by the sound of another aircraft coming from the same direction, so I stood up and started cheering. Why? Because every redblooded schoolboy knew that an enemy fighter over England would have a Spitfire on its tail. How wrong can you be? It was another rooftop ME109 virtually in the slipstream of the first. As it, too, banked away there followed another ME109 which then disappeared, leaving me - and Mr Evans, the master of 2A, shocked and puzzled. He had been about to get on his bicycle but abandoned it in the gutter while he, too, crouched and stared in disbelief. Three ME109s and no air raid warning or sign of the RAF.

Opposite the school entrance, in Hawthorn Grove, one of the shops down on the right-hand side had suffered damage from cannon fire - I found part of a shell in the gutter - but the 109s I saw did not appear to be firing their guns, and in any case were flying in the wrong direction. The cannon fire came from another enemy aircraft, a FockeWulf 190, which I did not see but was part of the same sortie. My brother Tony was in our flat at the time, looked out of a front window, saw the FW190 as it swooped over the house, heading south, and could also see the ME109s over Penge. My sister Margaret, who had just reached Thicket Road on her way home from school for lunch, remembers hearing gunfire and being taken into a house, away from the danger. There were no casualties in Penge that day but it was a far more tragic story a few miles - and in flying time a matter of seconds - away in Catford, where a 500lb bomb hit a school in Sandhurst Road, killing 38 children and six women teachers.

The aircraft which flew so low and so briefly into our lives were part of a larger group of ME109s and bomb-carrying FW190s, targeting South London and Maidstone, which took defensive forces completely by surprise, although three FW190s and four ME109s were shot down as they made their way back to France. That was little consolation for the grieving people in Catford.

Back to domestic matters - and this was the year that Nurse E.M. Martin, the district midwife, moved from number 14 to the flat below us at 19 - and with her came a wire-haired terrier called Monty. It also meant that her maroon Austin 7 Ruby - CMP616 (what a memory!) - was parked outside our place, ready to take her on regular rounds as well as emergencies. There was never any sign or mention of a husband, but Nurse Martin had an adopted son, Roy, on active service with the Queens Regiment as part of the 8th Army, soon to move from Africa to the European mainland.

The diminutive nurse immediately became a great friend of the family, especially my mother, with whom she shared all sorts of gossip. She also took delight in sharing her time off with us, taking Mum, Margaret and me on trips to the theatre. We saw Billy Cotton and his band at the Empress Theatre in Brixton, some variety shows at the Hippodrome in Croydon and a pantomime with Bud Flanagan at a theatre in The Strand, London. Her usual reaction on hearing good news regarding any of us: "VERY nice, too!"

Not so nice was the resumption of air raid warnings which started to interrupt our evenings. It was about this time that we first experienced the result of that Home Guard training on mysterious-looking guns, mentioned in Chapter 8.

Anti-aircraft defences now included "Z" Batteries of rocket launchers, manned by Home Guard members whose original task of helping to defeat invading Germans was not quite so vital now. Hitler's land forces were on the defensive in Russia and the Mediterranean area. The air raids were not as intensive or as frequent as those of the earlier Blitz, but it still meant decamping from our flat, hurrying along to the basement of number 13, and waiting for the All Clear. Occasionally we heard aircraft and gunfire; then one night came a very loud and drawn-out "Whoooosh!" It was not stuff coming down; it was stuff going up as the "Z" Battery near Anerley School went into action, although we did not know that at the time. The new and totally unexpected sound was frightening.

With acknowledgements to "The Blitz, Then and Now", a little additional information might help. "The 'Unrotating Projectile' or 'UP' rocket for short, had been developed before the war as a substitute for the shortage of anti-aircraft guns, the 3-inch solid-fuelled rocket approximating the performance of the 3.7-inch AA shell. One advantage was that they could be fired by fewer, less highly-trained men, but, against this had to be set the fact that the weapon was highly inaccurate. Nevertheless, the 'scattergun' approach was - for both friend and foe - an impressive psychological sight. The launchers fired salvoes of over 100 rockets at a time, which accelerated to 1,000mph in 1½ seconds before exploding simultaneously in a single, stupendous roar. The noise has been described as "rather like an express train passing through the living room, before crashing in the back garden". The experience was awesome, and it was this frightening noise that was to lead to the greatest tragedy of the Blitz.

This was on the evening of March 3 1943 at Bethnal Green tube station just north of the Thames and where, in nearby Victoria Park, a "Z" Battery had been established. The air raid warning sounded just after 8pm and many residents headed for the underground station which, like so many others, had become a shelter. As they crowded into the entrance, rockets were launched from Victoria Park, making the "stupendous roar" described in the previous paragraph. It caused widespread panic as people pressed towards the stairs leading to safety. A woman carrying a baby tripped, others fell over her - and still more fell as those outside, unaware of what had happened, kept pushing forward. Of the 173 people who died in the crush, 62 were children.

The tragedy was widely reported on BBC bulletins and in newspapers - but without mention of the anti-aircraft rockets. Their noise really was enough to cause panic - and it was no picnic, either, for the Home Guard gun crews. I recall Daphne Crabbe telling the family how her uncle, a sergeant with the battery near Anerley School, had given the order the first time it went into action. "He shouted 'Fire!' - and wondered what hit him."

All this must be seen as part of the background in a life containing so much else which seemed important at the time. Would I be able to go to the cinema this week? How could I fix the slow puncture in the front tyre of my faithful but ramshackle bike? Why am I good at English but hopeless at arithmetic? Will Mum have left a bucket of coal on the front steps at home, for me to carry up to our top flat? These and a thousand other random thoughts, usually during the twice-daily walk between home and the school in Oakfield Road.

On the way home at lunchtime there was always the chance that the baker's shop opposite the Town Hall would be selling bread rolls for a halfpenny. One of these, torn from a batch of a dozen or more, would have a firm brown top but soft sides. As you walked, grubby fingers plucked out the doughy inside and made several mouthfuls; that left a crusty shell to be gradually torn apart and consumed in small pieces. In that way, the roll could last a good quarter of a mile.

There was another baker's a little nearer the school, in Anerley Station Road, which never seemed to sell rolls but had more exotic offerings, well beyond the few coppers in my pocket. I could only look on when, one cold winter lunchtime with snow in the air, another boy went in and came out carrying a large tart topped with baked treacle. The sight was too much for one of his friends who made a grab at it. The tart slipped and fell to the ground - treacle side down. Its purchaser retrieved it amid an ominous silence and examined the broken pastry with its sweet - and dirt encrusted - covering, all the time muttering to himself, "You bastard...you bastard." Then he pushed the whole thing into the other lad's face and the two of them fell to the ground, fighting amid ever-increasing layers of dirt, pastry and treacle plus - and it could never have been better timed - a helping of snow. Bread rolls never caused that sort of trouble.

Children generally are always hungry, but the peak for me was on Friday afternoons when our class was marched from Oakfield Road to the Royston Playing Fields, one of the few pieces of land to escape the general "Dig for Victory" call and not be given over to growing vegetables. This one piece of open air exercise in the school week was never organised properly and while the few who had the ability or equipment managed to play football or cricket, most of us waited for "home time". This seemed much longer during the winter when, adding to the torture, the nearby Co-op bakery wafted the smell of freshly-cooked bread.

Walking to and from school twice a day must have totalled between four or five miles in reasonably clean air. Traffic was light and trolley buses using the stretch between Anerley Station Road and Thicket Road were, of course, electrically driven. So, we were fit enough - and at weekends or during lighter evenings our rattletrap bicycles gave additional exercise. Shoes which had not been outgrown gave good service, augmented by an occasional visit to the repair shop with its waxy smell of old dusty leather and polish, machines with revolving brushes, those iron feet known as “lasts” and shelves of footwear bearing labels which somehow linked them to the mender’s book and the prices charged.

At Oakfield there was a Boot Club, set up many years before by a benefactress, which added a penny to every shilling saved towards buying new footwear. The scheme operated through the school and was part of the morning routine in each class after the register had been called, in which pupils paid for that day’s milk (a penny) and/or school dinners (five pence). Money for National Savings and the Boot Club added to the teacher’s collection of coins, usually saved in suitably labelled Oxo tins. Shoe shops in the area would accept a letter of credit from the school. It is quite possible that the worthy lady who began the scheme not only wanted to encourage the saving habit but also ensure that money intended for children's boots did not find its way into the General Jackson or one of the many other pubs in Penge.

Yes, quite a number of boys still wore boots rather than shoes. They were better off than some of those who seemed to be stuck in Wellingtons, summer and winter, whether it was raining or not. The welly-wearing "schlick-schlock kids" could be heard approaching from a long way off and their legs appeared to have a permanent red ring just below the knee.

CHAPTER 10 - TONY'S NEAR-MISS

The start of 1943 meant that I would in the near future move from Class 1A, with the Churchill-worshipping Mr Letch, to Class 2A where Mr Evans conducted matters. This also meant a re-arrangement in Assembly, the morning ritual of lining up the whole school for prayers, announcements and a couple of hymns. Two lines of 1B pupils were at the front, with another two lines of 1A boys behind them. The same set-up followed for the other two streams, so that the deeper-voiced lads of 3A were at the back. Teachers for each form supervised their charges from the side of the hall and were adept at catching those boys who tended to faint, especially on winter mornings, before they hit the floor. The Church of England prayers (Roman Catholics went to a different school) were led by the headmaster, Mr Margham, and hymns were conducted by Mr Warren, who was in charge of Form 3A.

The business of gradually moving to the back of the hall was, I found, quite significant. At the end of summer and winter terms the final hymn was always "The Day Thou Gavest, Lord, is Ended" and meant that, at the age of 14, yet another batch of mixed-ability lads would be setting out in the working world with nothing more than a carefully-worded reference from Mr Margham to show for a total of nine years in the education system. I grew quite fond of Oakfield and used to joke that "if you could read and write when you left, they put your name on the honours board" - but there was a hint of truth behind the irony.

In the meantime, I had yet to acquire my first pair of long trousers and did not think too deeply about the future. My taste in reading matter broadened, and I looked more closely at some of the books available at home. In our front room was a dresser with shelves which held a mixture of volumes ranging from the heavily Roman story of Lytton's "Rienzi" to the Amazonian adventures of "Martin Rattler" by R.M. Ballantyne, together with the Penguin edition of "Aircraft Recognition" (essential if you wanted to know if that speck in the sky was one of ours) and a pocket-sized book on how to play football. These were just some of the subjects and titles in a strange mixture of more than two dozen which had become so familiar that they were largely ignored. Why did I not dip into "Adam in Moonshine" by J.B. Priestly?

One which turned out to be a delight was "Knotted Yarns" by Ashley Sterne - I hope the spelling is correct because the author would not have had anything to do with an actress of the same name in the 21st century. "Knotted Yarns" was a collection of crazy stories with titles like "Captain Joystick's Twilight Sleep" and "Caroline's Christmas." The latter tale was about the efforts of a titled but hard-up man to provide seasonal cheer for his baby daughter. Having burgled the Bank of England, he succeeded and then fell asleep on Christmas Eve. From what I can remember, the final lines read, "Nor did fortune allow Lord Whateveritwas to go unrewarded. He, too, found his stocking full; full of foot.

He had gone to bed with his boots on."

There was another part which described somebody receiving bad news. "On hearing this, he went completely to pieces. Bits of him fell into the fireplace and rolled into corners of the room…" I had never seen writing like this before. It was making fun of everyday language and taking the reader in new directions in much the same way as, a few years later, The Goons would do with words coming out of the radio.

Someone, I think it was Tony, made occasional additions to our home library. Three small volumes published by Methuen introduced me to the humorous work of Stephen Leacock, E.V. Knox and W.W. Jacobs, but there was a step towards darker matters with the arrival of two thickish black books of ghost stories. It was in one of these that I first read "Oh, Whistle, and I'll Come to You My Lad" by M.R. James, a classic horror tale which has since been filmed and televised but without getting anywhere near the impact that the written words can have on an active imagination. And what about the man who, in a derelict house, discovers an overcoat which turns out to be haunted and threatens him with eternal damnation? Or the desert island tale of a man and wife who gradually turn into weird sponges?

One of the surprises was to find that W.W. Jacobs, whose funny side had been displayed in one of the

Methuen volumes, was there in among the darker tales with "The Monkey's Paw" - another disturbing piece which has been filmed. Again, pictures on a screen can only take second place to the penmanship of a storyteller's skill - that of manipulating the reader's mind and reaching in to conjure up deeper demons.

It also happened that in 1943 the BBC began "Appointment With Fear", a really creepy late-night series which has never been equalled as an example of pure radio. The thirty-minute format played with the listeners' imagination, aided by the fact that the programme went out after 10pm and was introduced by Valentine Dyall's darkly menacing voice, with the addition of a distant bell chiming two chilling notes. Scripts by John Dickson Carr usually began the drama on a lighter note, setting scenes which gave the audience a false sense of security before gradually increasing the tension and edging into what were sometimes outlandishly macabre twists in the tale.

Take, for example, the programme in which two men had a bet that one of them would not spend the night alone in a locked room with a coffin which contained a dead body. The gloom was relieved by one candle which, by agreement, would last only two hours. Listeners shared the spoken thoughts - a sort of verbal diary - of the man whose vigil began with confidence but then, deeper into the night, began to waver. His voice strained as the candle threatened to gutter out before its scheduled time but did, in fact, go the two hours - but by then he was starting to babble in the near-blackness. Hysteria took over as he heard a noise which could only be the occupant of the coffin giving a series of three knocks against the lid...and then the horrific scream, "My God! It's getting out!" (At this point, radio listeners would be glancing uneasily over their shoulders.) The twist in this particular tale was that the coffin's occupant - obviously not dead - while aiming to give the watcher a real fright had gone too far and scared him, literally, to death. As a result, it was he who found himself locked in a room with a body.

Not convinced? The acting and production on "Appointment With Fear" was in the best tradition of BBC drama at the time. My mother, whose sense of humour always bordered on the devilish, once dared me to listen to an episode of the programme in our front room, alone and by firelight. I am not ashamed to say that after twenty minutes, as the horrific pay-off approached, I switched on the light.

What else was happening at home? My brother Tony, senior by four years, had actually been seen walking in the company of a girl - the first of many - but also continued as a member of 1903 (Penge) Squadron Air Training Corps, which meant spending at least one evening each week at the headquarters in Croydon Road and attending Sunday morning parades. He also played for the unit's football team which, to be the best of my knowledge, never managed to win a game.

The addition of drums and trumpets to the squadron's equipment sparked a more active interest in music. Tony had bought a second-hand gramophone, together with a selection of records, and enjoyed listening to the jazzy work of Artie Shaw, Benny Goodman and others. He even dabbled, unsuccessfully, with the clarinet. His ATC-issued trumpet eventually produced better results, probably because those used in the band were valveless, slightly lower toned than a bugle, but still having the same five-note restriction in the range of notes available. After a certain amount of training, the squadron's trumpets and drums could kick up a version of "All For a Shilling a Day" among other tunes to accompany its occasional marches. It was a year or two before Tony bought a conventional trumpet and by then his hero was Harry James. At the same time a chap named Maguigan, from Royston Road, used to turn up on Saturday afternoons and give music lessons.

Tony enjoyed the ATC because it provided companionship with young men of his age, plus occasional adventures such as flights in RAF planes when 1903 Squadron visited airfields. The service was keen on attracting young men because at that time the constant bombing of Germany was proving costly in numbers of lost aircrews.

Among the active service stations which hosted ATC squadrons was Tangmere on the West Sussex coast which provided a few memorable moments for Tony and other members of his unit. There was the misty afternoon when Tony and his close friend Ken Baxter walked to the local village. It meant taking a long, straight road with no houses, parallel to the main runway. They could hear a single aircraft circling slowly and guessed by the engine sound that it was probably a Fairey Swordfish, the open-cockpit biplane still very much in use by the RAF and Royal Navy for anti-submarine patrols. Nicknamed the "Stringbag", this relatively unsophisticated plane also served as a workhorse and runaround.

The pilot of this one was trying to work out the difference between Tangmere's landing strip and the public road - as Tony and Ken realised when the Swordfish appeared ahead of them out of the mist, low down and coming in their direction, showing every sign of preparing to land on the public highway. Both cadets waved frantically and pointed towards the runway, the other side of a high wire mesh fence. Obligingly, the aircraft climbed a few feet and, as it slowly chugged past, the pilot waved back in thanks. This flying operation was obviously part of a special mission - on one of the lower wings the Swordfish carried a large suitcase while the fuselage between the cockpit and tailplane was encumbered with a roped-on bicycle.

There was one other narrow escape, this time involving ATC cadets from a squadron based in the Liverpool area and having their annual camp at Tangmere at the same time as the boys from Penge. One rainy afternoon it was decided to stage an inter-squadron boxing tournament in the gymnasium - setting lads of approximately the same height and weight against each other for one round. These unskilled events earned the name "blood baths" and tended to prove that, for novice boxers, three minutes is a very long time when spent in the close company of the wrong person.

Tony regarded himself as reasonably fit and able to stay out of trouble. In the initial line-up he was opposite a cadet he later described as "dusky-looking" and was not too worried, even when told that the other lad's brother was champion of the Royal Navy. However, a few minutes before he was due to fight Tony was asked to stand down because someone else, a little nearer his opponent's weight, was "keen to have a scrap." So it was a chance to sit back and watch his replacement climb into the ring. Less than a minute later, the guy "keen to have a scrap" was flat on his back and unconscious, while Tony realised that he had only just missed being on the wrong end of a severe thumping.

The "dusky-looking" cadet, who had handed out all the punishment, was Randolph Turpin who would go on to win the world middleweight title from Sugar Ray Robinson in 1951. His brother Dick, who served in the Royal Navy, also became a successful professional boxer, but it was Randolph who for a short time found fame and fortune. His downward spiral is one of boxing's most tragic stories.

The RAF was always very much in the news in 1943 especially when, on the night of May 16th-17th, bombers raided the German dams which, we were told, provided the Ruhr's industries with electrical power.

Wing Commander Guy Gibson, who led the operation, became an instant hero and was honoured by the BBC who chose him as one of Roy Plomley's guests on "Desert Island Discs." I listened to the programme but cannot remember any of the records he played apart from the RAF March Past by Walford Davies which I suppose he was pretty well obliged to include.

Tony would never take to the air as a member of the RAF because by the time his call-up came, the war was over and - ironically - he would not have been accepted into the RAF because he tested as colour-blind. Instead, he became a soldier with the Royal Engineers and spent most of his time at the Staff College in Camberley, Surrey, working on the production of maps. In later life his printing work included supervising the production of brightly-illustrated shopping catalogues but in the eyes of the service medics he was still - officially - colour-blind. Who decided? It was probably the same people who decided that a deaf and dumb man could go on firewatch.

With the arrival of warm weather in 1943 the youngsters in our part of Thicket Road added swimming to their activities. None of us was ever taught properly; it was a matter of going to the local swimming baths on a Saturday, getting used to the water, the smell of chlorine, the splashing and noise, then gradually developing a method of getting away from the crowded shallow end without actually drowning. My first experience of swimming baths had been before the war when Uncle Dan, serving with the army in India, spent an extended UK leave with us in 1938 and took Tony and me to the public baths at Forest Hill. I went in once - and panicked at the unexpected pressure of the water against my chest. Tony seemed all right and Uncle Dan, very fit and apt to show off, swam and performed fancy dives from the top board.

The next time I tried swimming was in 1941 when my brother and I were evacuated to Exeter. Tony spent most of his off-school time with his friend "Fritz" Germany while I discovered an indoor pool not far from the hairdresser's shop kept by my foster mother and her two daughters. Oddly enough, I did not learn to swim there but I used to like diving and developed a technique of taking a header in at the deep end, cutting across the right-angle where the side of the pool met the end. By judging the distance properly it was possible to dive in, come up and grab the rail. This never struck me as dangerous, even when another lad pushed me in at the deep end and, as I was going down, thought "He doesn't know I can't swim!" Fortunately I was able to improvise a couple of strokes and get to the rail - and the experience never put me off.

Back in Anerley and still unable to swim, I found a book in the local library with a title like "Teach Yourself to Swim" or "Swimming Can Be Fun!" which appeared to be the answer. The first chapter, however, was not too encouraging.

It asked, "How often do you go swimming?" and went on, "Let's say that you go to the pool six times each week - and leave it on Sunday, just for a rest." Six days a week? Whoever wrote that was not aware of people like us who were lucky if they managed to go once a fortnight. It meant persuading Mum to give you sixpence - a penny for the bus ride from the Crooked Billet to Beckenham Baths, fourpence to get in and a penny for the return journey. Two or three of us would walk the length of Thicket Road to the Penge end, turn right and continue under the two railway arches down past St John's Church to the pub where a 227 single decker was waiting.

In the summer there was usually a queue to get into the baths - plural because there was more than one. The first class was larger and had a gallery for spectators but part of its glass roof was lost because of air raids and whatever had replaced it made the place darker. The bath there could also be boarded over for dances and other public functions, so it was only occasionally available to swimmers. Second class was smaller and brighter. In the dressing room a man in a booth handed out wire baskets to store clothes and towel; you gave it back and had to remember its number.

On the other side of the footbath lay chlorinated chaos. Most of the Saturday swimmers were youngsters, naturally noisy, with the sound seemingly amplified by the bare walls and glass roof. During hot weather, when the place was exceptionally busy, your visit would only last twenty minutes. The attendant controlled this by blowing his whistle and shouting the numbers on the clothes baskets - "All those from 51 to 70 - out now!" The system worked reasonably well and I only saw one defiant boy who eventually gave in when threatened with having his clothes thrown into the pool.

Drying and dressing also involved the question of whether to indulge in the luxury of getting a blob of Brylcreem from a dispensing machine which charged a penny. That would mean having to walk all the way home - but it didn't seem so bad because there was usually plenty to talk about with your friends. "I jumped from the TOP board!" and "I swam half a length under water!" We felt a little fresher, too, for at least an hour as we walked towards Penge, carrying our swimming trunks wrapped in a damp towel which smelled of chlorine. The same smell clung to us and, having no doubt swallowed some of the water, we even burped chlorine as well.

So when did I actually learn to swim? I cannot remember; it was mainly a question of gaining confidence and trying to copy those who could manage breast-stroke or crawl, then realising that if you breathed properly your body stayed on the surface.

If we felt like going further afield and staying longer than twenty minutes there was always the open air pool at Brockwell Park, not far from Brixton, and requiring a bus ride there and back. One of the London lidos - there was another at Tooting Bec - Brockwell Park's facility seemed huge compared with Beckenham baths. There was also a barrage balloon unit in the park and it sometimes seemed that those in charge of the balloon deliberately caused its shadow to eclipse the sun and make the inevitable queue seem colder. Once in, you could stay as long as you liked but the actual experience never lived up to the expectation. Yes, the pool was big and surrounded by a wide paved area for sunbathing, but the water was unheated and swimming was not as much fun as Beckenham where cramming as much activity as you could into twenty minutes added a strange sort of zest to the experience.

I was never sorry to leave Brockwell Park and wait for the bus - No. 2 - while also watching the trams clanging their way through to Brixton and Herne Hill. On one late afternoon return trip to Crystal Palace I sat behind the unbelievably lovely Madge Hunt and thought, "She has to take the bus home after work!" Why was I so surprised?

CHAPTER 11 - EVERLASTING SUNDAYS

Earlier in this narrative I have referred to other people in Thicket Road who played an occasional part in our lives. There were also a few "friends of friends" from elsewhere in Penge and Anerley who became familiar, in particular the Cooks and the Barbers who may have been related to our close neighbours, the Shipstones.

The Cooks lived in one of the many terraced houses in Hawthorn Grove - not the classiest part of Penge although the family put on a carefully-managed air of respectability. The father, Bert Cook, had an office job with Olby's, the builders' merchant and hardware store in Penge High Street. By 1943 he was in the RAF and appeared occasionally in uniform with three stripes on his sleeve.

The mother - whose name I cannot recall - always called Mrs Shipstone "Eve", which indicated a long association, and on her regular visits to the flat at number 13a was sometimes accompanied by her younger daughter Barbara, a year or two older than Beryl Shipstone. There was also an older daughter, Joyce, and a son named Cyril who was in his late teens, good looking, athletic and seemed to be regarded as the hope of the family. Mrs Cook was sociable enough but liked to give the impression of being slightly more worldly than the other mothers around her.

The Barbers provided something of a contrast. They lived in a council house on the corner of Oak Grove Road and Ash Grove, the far side of Croydon Road and the Robin Hood. It seemed a long distance away and must have felt even further for John Barber, the youngest and about the same age as Dennis and I, who I recall arriving at 13a Thicket Road one rainy night a year or two before 1943. He was soaking wet and crying, having walked from his home in order to borrow a penny for the gas meter. I am still not sure how many there were in the Barber family. John seemed to have a fair selection of older brothers and sisters as well as a tubby, garrulous mother who, like Mrs Cook, also called Mrs Shipstone "Eve". We never saw anything of Mr Barber - Herbert - until some time later; but that will have to wait. I do recall my mother laughing at the story of how one of the older brothers, who had a job helping to dig air raid shelters in back gardens, was overheard talking to a workmate during a pause in the laborious task of cutting through the London clay behind our house. Wiping away the sweat, he said, "Y'know what? I keep my bloody family" - with heavy emphasis on the "keep". The Barber finances were never stable - as shown by the wet-trek-for-a-penny incident.

Somehow, not by any advance arrangement, there were occasional afternoon gatherings of these and other acquaintances in our large front room, when the tea and conversation flowed between Mum and Mrs Shipstone, joined by the Cooks or Barbers and other assorted near-neighbours including Daphne Crabbe, Mrs Sims, Mrs

Jacobs, all holding forth in a generally light-hearted way on the current war news, local scandals or even what was available in shops. I always enjoyed listening and scrounging a cup of tea until the one step on the stairway that was guaranteed to set every visitor hastily gathering up their belongings - handbag, gas mask, odd bits of shopping - and making a hasty exit. The step, usually supplemented by a cough, signalled the arrival of "the Old Man", my father, of whom most visitors seemed afraid. He would be met on the stairs by a bunch of departing women and find my mother clearing up teacups from a room empty of people and the friendly, chatty atmosphere of just a minute or two before. I always felt sorry when this happened - not for those leaving our flat, but for my father. Surely he must have noticed the effect he had?

This re-establishment of the traditional man-of-the-house reigning over the rest of us could well have been due to the progress of the war. The Blitz, which brought everyone together, was now long gone, and there were only occasional "nuisance" air raids because Germany was far too occupied in Russia and the Mediterranean to waste aircraft elsewhere. So, family life had begun to settle into a near-normal pattern, including the Sunday afternoon routine in which Dad, having returned from his lunchtime pub session, would have his lunch and settle in an armchair by the fireplace with a cup of tea nearby.

He would then tune the radio in to a station broadcasting opera - the heavier and more Germanic the better - and fall asleep with his head on the arm of the chair. The tea remained untouched. This rendered the front room a no-go zone for the rest of the family who had to make do by retreating to the kitchen or one of the bedrooms. The opera was loud and seemingly interminable while Dad, slumped in the armchair, was fast asleep and his tea went cold. If anyone crept into the room and tried to turn the radio down, he was instantly awake and objecting, "I was listening to that!" Attempted removal of the scummy tea brought a similar result: "I'll drink that in a minute!" He never did - and those who were fed up with sitting on kitchen chairs would, weather permitting, go for a walk or seek the company of nearby friends.

On the subject of friends, Tony by this time had his first (as far as we knew) girlfriend. Her name was Joan Bale, and she lived with her family, including a couple of sisters, in Palace Road. I met up with the sisters two or three years later in the shorthand class at Penge Evening Institute. Joan worked in Woolworth's in Westow Hill, Upper Norwood, and was a good-looking brunette who still kept in touch with the family even after she and Tony stopped seeing each other. He went on to have a whole succession of "birds", most of whom came to tea on a Sunday after Dad had relinquished his front room armchair.

Tony's membership of the ATC continued and he was also interested in photography as well as drawing and painting, all of which were connected with his apprenticeship in photo-gravure printing. The availability of film sheets at work enabled him to load the plates used by one of his first cameras and he even started to develop and print pictures at home. A number of these appeared to be self-portraits and one in particular featured his face superimposed on an illustration of an airman in full flying kit. He had "borrowed" the picture from a magazine in which it was used to illustrate the items of kit used by an RAF crew member. Numbers had been superimposed on the photograph, explained in the caption with "1 - Oxygen mask" and so on, but Tony had painted these out - or so he thought. One or two people were impressed with my brother's flying ace image until someone asked why the number 16 appeared on his body.

Drawing and painting skills, which would last a lifetime, continued with some graphic wartime images although many of these were unfinished. One illustration he did complete was a commission from Dad on behalf of a contact, possibly Sid Legge, with the old Crystal Palace Company. This was a small black and white line drawing of the old Crystal Palace to accompany part of a presentation. The detail proved quite difficult and Tony had several attempts before his completed work was described by Dad as "brilliant". It was, too.

And what about Margaret? My little sister was six years old and spending a lot of time with Beryl Shipstone - a friendship which would last many years - as well as being increasingly useful to Mum in the running of errands. This sometimes meant being sent to Knights, the grocer's shop, armed with a ration book in which it was difficult to tell whether the Points had been previously crossed out. As has been previously explained, many tinned and pre-packed items were not strictly rationed although obtaining them meant giving up part of each person's regular allocation of Points. Shop assistants didn't bother to cut them out of the ration book but marked them heavily with an indelible pencil although - and other housewives noticed this - some pencils were not so indelible as others and the Points could be restored with the careful use of a hard rubber. How many of these dodgy-looking ration books were proffered by innocent children? Margaret was also friends with the Hughes family, now fully restored with the return of "Poppa" Hughes from wherever he had been since the stripping incident in Anerley Road. They went to church on Sunday - not to St Paul's in Hamlet Road but more than half a mile farther, along Aukland Road to St John's where the Church of England establishment had distinctly Romish tendencies. "Father" Eric Bailey was in charge; there was lots of genuflecting and incense-loaded processions. St John's was in a well-heeled area.

Mr Hughes took his family to church in a rather presentable Austin (where did he get the petrol?), so the novelty of a car ride also appealed to Margaret who went along in her straw bonnet to attend the Sunday school, having first begged "a penny for Jesus" from Dad as he settled down for that notorious, post-lunch Wagner-fuelled snooze. Good for Margaret; that was one way of escaping.

CHAPTER 12 - ACRES OF BLACKBERRIES

What else happened to us in 1943? At Oakfield School I moved up from 1A to 2A and was sorry to lose the daily instruction from Mr Letch as well as his devotion to Winston Churchill and the occasional story about past events at the school. One of these concerned a boy who, at some time in the 1930s, had been eating sandwiches during the lunch break. Tommy Letch noticed that they were not the usual brown bread doorsteps-and-dripping but well cut with white bread and wrapped in a rather superior kind of paper napkin. The boy, proudly, announced that they were royal sandwiches, prepared for the King of Spain (or was it Italy or some other European country?). Anyway, they were definitely royal and their intended consumer had left them on the boat train travelling into Victoria station. The boy's father, employed by Southern Railway as a steward or perhaps a guard, picked up the unwanted snack and took it home where it was passed on to his son - which is how a lad in class 1A at Oakfield School came to be lunching on royal sandwiches. Stranger things have happened!

I think 1943 was also the year of Mum's blackberrying expedition into the Crystal Palace grounds, originally an area of more than 300 acres which had been closed to the public since the early days of the war. From the top deck of any 654 trolleybus waiting at the top of Anerley Hill it was possible to see evidence of some activity - lines of parked vehicles which never seemed to go anywhere or serve any useful purpose - but that was about all. These cars and vans were a constant temptation to some of the more adventurous local youngsters and there was at least one juvenile court case resulting from an expedition into the forbidden grounds. Kids managed to get some of the cars going and were driving them around before being nabbed by the palace ground staff.

Keepers were still being watchful when Mum, who knew the Crystal Palace Company secretary Sid Legge, and his wife, obtained a pass to the grounds and was let in through a gate on Crystal Palace Parade. She carried a basket and was accompanied by Margaret and one of our neighbours, a young woman from the Hone family next door. As expected, years of neglect had let the brambles run riot and there were plenty of blackberries waiting to be picked. Mum was also fascinated by the overall look of a place which had been familiar territory in the past - close to Thicket Road and accessible for family rambles.

Mum and her friend wandered into the acres and were gathering blackberries when there was a shout - an angry-sounding “Hoi!” - from the distance. Two or three hundred yards away an irate keeper was stomping through the bushes and heading in their direction with a meaningful air. This was not the right way to approach my mother, who continued to gather fruit as if nothing had happened. A little nearer and another “Hoi!” - but it had no effect; Mum still picked the blackberries. Eventually the keeper emerged through the bushes, red-faced from dodging his way through the brambles and - possibly - from the sheer cheek of this woman and her companions who appeared not to take any notice of him.

"You're not allowed in here!" raved the keeper.

"Aren't I?" said Mum, still collecting the blackberries.

"How did you get in?"

"Through the gate," replied Mum.

"You're supposed to have special permission!"

"Do you mean this?" Mum paused in her fruit-gathering and produced the piece of paper from Sid Legge.

The keeper snatched it from her and then saw that it was indeed a proper pass into the grounds, signed by his boss. The change in demeanour, from outrage to fawning politeness, was comic. The man managed to summon a sickly smile as he returned the paper. "Oh...that'll be *quite* all right," he cringed.

"I thought so," said Mum, turning her attention back to the blackberry bushes.

She probably had a lot more to say and no doubt would have let the keeper know about it in no uncertain terms, but for the presence of her young daughter and the neighbour. It all ended in sweetness - thanks to a seasonal extra ration of sugar for jam-making, granted by the Ministry of Food.

Unlike some of the other lads in the neighbourhood, I never ventured into the grounds of the Crystal Palace during the war years but I was always intrigued by what could be seen, as I have mentioned, from the top deck of a trolleybus. In addition, the windows at the rear of our flat in Thicket Road gave glimpses of odd buildings including what, for a long time, I took to be a church tower. It was topped by a lantern fitting - unlit, of course - which remained in place for a long time until it was finally dislodged. A church in the Palace grounds? It was, as I later found, a remnant from the Empire Exhibition of 1912 which had featured a scaled-down version of the Canadian Government buildings in Ottawa. After 30-plus years, only the tower survived, but it was a tribute to whoever had set up its strong timber frame, faced with a lath-and-plaster finish which carried a recognisable representation of the real building's exterior. When the grounds were first opened immediately after the war I managed to get inside, climbed almost to the top and felt the structure swaying in the wind. It was all rather alarming, so I descended! Shortly afterwards the whole thing was taken down as attempts were made to clear the Palace grounds.

Thinking back to the early 1930s, when my brother Tony and I first explored all those acres - before the fire of 1936 - it seemed even then that the grounds were past their best and lacked proper care. There were rusty pipes leading to water features that no longer worked, broken-down fences, gone-to-seed grasslands and outbuildings on the verge of collapse. And yet the management had built a road racing circuit in 1937 in an attempt, perhaps, to bring back the crowds. It was a move which succeeded on the days when race meetings were held - but the year-round attraction was still lacking. I still have the greatest affection for those acres - but my immediate task is to write about the family and 1943.

Towards the end of the summer that year, Dad, Mum, Margaret and I went on holiday - but not to Eastbourne, which had always been the place I associated with a summer break. We set off for London and made our way to Liverpool Street, a terminus I had never seen before and found to be far more full of smoke from railway locomotives than the familiar Victoria, served by largely electrified lines from the suburbs and south coast. Liverpool Street seemed scruffier, with more than the usual mix of uniformed men and women from the armed services. The carriage that took us in a northerly direction was a different colour from the familiar green of Southern Railways - was it LNER? I cannot remember. We changed once, I think, on to a branch line and arrived at Widford in Hertfordshire.

The weather was not very friendly, with occasional spots of rain as the four of us trooped uphill from the station towards what turned out to be a small village with a couple of shops and a pub called The Green Man. Somebody must have given us directions and we set off up what appeared to be a very long lane, past a group of houses and then heading towards open country. Our luggage, shared among us, seemed to get heavier with every step. Dad, who was leading the way, had said something about camping, so it was a relief when I saw the top of a bell tent above the hedge further up the lane on the right. There was also a house with a thatched roof - and a few minutes later we had arrived at The Rick, home of the Kelly family.

Mr and Mrs Kelly had a growing family with a son, Roger, six or seven years old, and a daughter. Jan, three or four. Both addressed their parents as Reg and Miriam (or “Mim”), which seemed overly familiar to me, and there was no trace of rural or countryfied accents. Reg was on the staff of a technical college in London and travelled to town every working day. Both he and his wife appeared to be prematurely grey and had a relaxed approach to life. The Rick, with its two dogs - black Labradors Jock and Molly - surrounded by an assortment of goats, chickens, a cow and a pony plus a 13-acre cornfield was indeed a very friendly place. The Goldsmiths were not the only family on holiday there; a short distance from the house was a permanently-sited caravan with an assortment of youngsters and their mother, who came from north London.

The bell tent, it turned out, was rather leaky. We found this during the one and only night that the Goldsmiths spent under canvas After that we transferred to spare rooms in the main house and I was in the lounge, sleeping on a large settee near a full-size concert grand piano. Despite its modern build with running water and an up-to-date bathroom, the Rick had no mains gas or electricity and relied on paraffin for cooking and lighting. Lanterns with wicks and glass cones were a portable novelty in the way they supplied an adequate light with a comforting glow; slow-burning cookers with wicks provided some heat in the kitchen but for the speedier tasks such as boiling a kettle or a pot the household relied on Primus stoves which could be temperamental.

It was in the kitchen at breakfast times that Margaret and I first tasted the delights of porridge made with goat's milk. It was a delightfully creamy novelty - and the Kellys gave us generous portions. There must have been other items for Mum and Dad but I don't really remember. It underlined the difference between urban living and being close to the land. That may sound exaggerated but, as I have said elsewhere, what reached the table in our Anerley flat was there as a result of Mum's daily juggling with ration books and hunting, along with other housewives, for what was available in local shops. For a few precious days on a small farm in Hertfordshire there was extra food on the doorstep, eggs that didn't have to be treated like gold dust and milk without having to look down the road in the morning and hope that the delivery from United Dairies would not be late.

The war was still with us, of course. Not far from Widford was Hunsdon with an RAF station from which flew Mosquitos, the "wooden wonder" aircraft whose twin engines provided an occasional background noise. But when it came to actual war news I was surprised to find that the household did not have a radio. There was no mains electricity, but other people in the same situation had battery-driven radios. Did the Kellys, perhaps, want to keep war news away from the children? I was not too bothered about it; after all, we would all be back in south London within a week or two and the news during August and September continued to be good as the Allies, with North Africa done and dusted, invaded Sicily and then attacked the Italian mainland. That country's Fascist leader, Mussolini, had already been overthrown on July 25 which proved The Beano comic right: Musso the Wop was indeed a Bigga-da Flop.

On our holiday there was plenty to keep Margaret and me amused. With the other children from the caravan we explored the fields, hedges and haystacks, had an occasional day out by walking into Widford and catching a bus to Ware or Bishop's Stortford, or gave a hand looking after the goats. This involved taking them from their enclosure and finding spots to which individual animals could be tethered and then spend their day nibbling at the nearby hedge. Under supervision we could even try our hand at milking - goats being less intimidating than a hefty-looking cow.

Mum and Dad's sleeping arrangements took some time to sort out. Before eventually finding a place in the house they tried spending the night in an outhouse made of straw bales but gave it up as a bad idea when Dad awoke to find that Mum was being attacked by a rat. Socially they found a welcome at the Green Man pub in the village where the landlady earned Mum's admiration by being able to whistle while she worked and at the same time keep a cigarette going in the corner of her mouth.

Back at The Rick the main field's corn harvest had been gathered before we arrived and the sheaves, dried in stooks, were in a neatly-built corn stack, complete with a temporary thatched roof, awaiting the threshing machine. A pause here for those who think that farmers have always used combine harvesters which tackle a field of corn (or wheat or barley) and produce the grain in one fell swoop. At the time of which I am writing, a field of corn would first be tackled by a tractor towing a cutter and binder which spat out sheaves held together by a special twine. The sheaves had then to be picked up by hand and placed in stooks of six or more sheaves, supporting each other with the cut ends of the stalks at the bottom, leaving the ears of corn to dry at the upper end. "Stooking" - that is picking up the sheaves in pairs (one under each arm) and standing them together before adding another two or three pairs, is backbreaking work. But find an old picture of a newly-cut field with neat lines of stooks and you will be looking at one of the lost treasures of farming.

The next stage - weather permitting - was collection of the dry sheaves from their stooks and using pitchforks to load them onto a harvest cart which took the sheaves to a spot where they could be built into a stack and wait for the thresher. Small farms had to take their turn with this machine. It was belt-driven by power from a tractor and took a team of at least half a dozen people to keep the operation going. It was dangerous, too, with pitchforks tossing up a continuous supply of sheaves to those on top of the thresher who had the job of cutting and getting rid of the binder twine, loosening up the stalks and dropping them into an opening. They had to be quick and careful; there were stories of inattentive people who lost limbs as a result of falling into the machine.

There was plenty of noise: from the tractor supplying the power, from the machine itself, from the shouting of instructions and warnings. The air was also full of dust as chaff and straw were spat out. And the grain itself? That was being graded and fed into sacks at the business end of the thresher; the real business and the whole reason behind this complicated and labour-intensive process. I know that we are now blessed with combine harvesters but I am still glad that I saw the way it was done in the 1940s and can understand the feeling of "harvest home" that the workers then must have felt as they washed away the sweat and dust of a long day.

Within a day or two the field of stubble was put to the plough (I think that's the term) by a man driving a machine with caterpillar tracks. He sat on the tractor and had levers each side of him with which to steer it. This interesting process was made slightly comical whenever he caught sight of Mrs Kelly or any other woman. An inherently polite and cheerful pipe-smoker, he would raise his hat and take the pipe out of his mouth - a two-handed task which meant letting go of the steering levers for a couple of hazardous seconds before pipe and hat were both replaced.

When he wasn't working in London, Mr Kelly always had a list of jobs around the farm. I was helping him with a task which involved a concrete mixer - a great novelty as far as I was concerned - when Mrs Kelly arrived with a welcome tray of tea and announced, "Mrs Goldsmith says it is quite all right for Alan to stay another week." It was news to me but I accepted the chance while at the same time wondering how I would catch up with school work. Then the thought occurred that during September a large number of other pupils would also be missing, earning money with their families while working in the hop fields of Kent. Another thought: I would have to travel back to Anerley on my own - providing an adventurous end to the rural holiday.

Mum, Dad and Margaret went back; then a week later, feeling independent and confident, I set off towards Widford with my few belongings in a knapsack.

Some men half way down the lane asked, "Where are you off to?" and, thinking they wouldn't know Penge or Anerley, I replied, "Crystal Palace." They seemed impressed. "Got a long way to go," one of them said. But I had my instructions; to get the train at Widford, change at one of the larger stations and get the connection to Liverpool Street. I was familiar with the London Underground system and could make my way to Stockwell, then catch a bus to the top of Anerley Hill. Within a couple of hours I was home again and wondering what Class 2A at Oakfield School would be like under Mr Evans.

CHAPTER 13 - A WHOOSH AND A FLASH

My new form master was already familiar through taking the twice-weekly physical training classes. During a school week there were a few specialised activities for which we moved from our usual classroom: PT was in the main hall with Mr Evans in charge; also in the hall we had singing with Mr Warren; in a separate room was art with Mr Rodwell; and most of us looked forward to the one morning or afternoon each week spent in the woodwork centre with Mr Love.

As a form teacher Mr Evans was much more vocal and opinionated than the older Mr Letch in 1A. He also liked to use shock tactics, as in the dreaded first session each Thursday afternoon when we tackled algebra. We had barely settled down when, without even removing his cycle clips, Mr Evans was bellowing, "X shillings; how many pounds?" and "X pounds; how many shillings?" The answers were, respectively, "X over 20" and "20X" but most of the class were still thinking about lunch - good or bad - and were hardly ready to get their heads around problems and equations. It has to be faced, however, there were thirty or more boys in that class with little chance for individual attention or coaching.

Thursday afternoon was the worst part of the week. There was hardly time to think about algebraic equations

- plus multiplied by plus means plus; minus multiplied by minus means plus; plus multiplied by minus equals minus - before we headed into the main hall where Mr Warren's singing classes called for special attention to diction and a crisp delivery of songs in unison. We never ventured into the realms of descants or anything complicated but did our best with "Who Is Sylvia?" and "On Wings of Song". I was disappointed that our class never got round to "The Earl King" which others had performed while Mr Warren, an excellent pianist, played the darkly thrilling accompaniment written by Schubert.

The final session on Thursday was first aid, a mixture of theory and practical demonstrations which should have been interesting and useful but somehow failed to be either. We learned the names and locations of pressure points and were shown how to make a sling for an injured arm but - again, because of class numbers - there was never the opportunity for hands-on practice. It was all written into an exercise book, chucked into the desk and left as the class ended and boys headed for home.

There were good days and bad days at school. Mr Evans was popular with most of the lads, although I always felt that there was a hidden and less trustworthy side to all his bluster. Nevertheless, he encouraged toy and model making in our spare time so that towards the end of the year we could stage a sale to other classes with the aim of raising money for the RAF. The £20 total would pay, we were told, for a dinghy which could save the crew of a bomber if it had to "ditch" in the sea. Another plus was the class party at Christmas for which everyone was invited to bring home-made treats and spend an afternoon singing, joking, and discovering whose mother was best at producing cakes.

End of term grew nearer, without any suggestion of exams or reports. I could remember being with my mother in Oakfield Road several years earlier and watching huge-looking boys from the school on their way home at the end of term, opening envelopes which contained their exam results and comments from teachers. Critical papers were posted down the nearest drain - and never mind about the accompanying slip which required a parental signature to prove that a report had actually been delivered home. We never had any reports to deliver, good or bad. For many of us in 2A there was only a year to go before the headmaster, Mr Margham, wrote references and the wide world received another batch of 14-year-olds.

Back at 19 Thicket Road, the diminutive and ever-friendly Nurse Martin seemed to enjoy having the Goldsmith family as fellow tenants and kept my mother fully informed of all the events involving families who needed her services. Being a midwife and district nurse meant that she and her trusty Austin Ruby would disappear at any hour of the day or night and yet she still had time to take Mum, Margaret, and me to the theatre occasionally.

In addition to all this, Nurse Martin devoted some of her attention to her wirehaired terrier, Monty, who got lucky one afternoon when Mum and Margaret, on their way to the top flat, were met on the half-way landing by their downstairs neighbour, standing at her kitchen door and offering a cup of tea. The hospitality was gladly accepted and Margaret was also given a jam tart. She nibbled her way round the pastry edges, saving the jam part as a final treat - and then dropped it. Monty didn't waste the opportunity.

The dog was also responsible for a change in what Mum, Margaret, and I did when an air raid warning sounded. There were five in the family, of course, but Dad had duties as a Civil Defence warden and by this time Tony was old enough at 17 to be a CD messenger. In the past, we three would have gone along to the Shipstone family in the basement at number 13, but now that would have meant leaving Nurse Martin - who had to be within earshot of the telephone - on her own. Another change was that German raids did not seem to be like the all-night blitzes of 1940-41 but lasted only an hour or two. The result was that four of us, plus the dog, would leave our respective flats, go downstairs and wait in the hall of number 19 because - and Nurse Martin was adamant in this - the dog felt safe there.

I did not feel safe and will explain why. The hall was a communal entrance for three flats and its double doors (we only ever used one) were both partially glazed. The entrance was at the top of two flights of stone steps and faced the open street at a height of about 20 feet. There was also a glass transom. In addition, it was cold and we had nowhere to sit - but out of loyalty to Nurse Martin and because her dog felt safe, we stood there during air raids. Others in the house, the Blakes in the basement and those who lived on the first floor, stayed behind their doors and were probably safer than the rest of us.

I have no clear recollection of the Christmas and New Year period as 1943 gave way to 1944. It may have been the festive season at which a consignment of soft toys arrived from Australia for distribution through the local junior schools. The "Penge and Anerley News" carried a picture of joyful youngsters clutching their gifts and cheering the generosity of people from the other side of the world. The photographer, Peter Eastment, also took a close-up shot of Margaret holding her doll and that, too, appeared with the caption: "Thank you, Australia, says this little girl from Anerley." As the reporter and caption writer, Dad thought that he could hardly include his own daughter's name.

Each gift carried a tag with the donor's name and address but I doubt if any letters of thanks were sent. Australia seemed a long way off but it did plant the thought that perhaps one day in the future I would go and maybe even work there.

What sort of work? In one of those just-back-from-the-pub Saturday evenings Dad had asked his 13-year-old younger son whether there were any thoughts about what

Sunshine from Down Under on a snowy day! My sister Margaret (right) with a war-time gift from Australia, one of many which cheered up children, seen below, at Anerley School.

to do after leaving school. "Something in the same line as you," I replied, not really having any great ideas to offer but being aware that my strongest subject at school was English, which helped to express thoughts for that weekly exercise known as "Composition." The conversation with Dad went no further, or so I thought.

Christmas had provided its usual wartime fare of a free Saturday morning show for children at the Rialto cinema in Upper Norwood, a few paper chains in the main room of our flat, one of Mum's miracle dinners with a pudding (made in November) and lots of enforced jollity from the BBC Home Service and Forces programmes interrupted by the seasonal worldwide tour of the Commonwealth leading up to the King's faltering broadcast. It was, of course, not the last Christmas of the Second World War. There would be one other, about which I wrote an article many years later for a magazine produced by a newspaper group in Canterbury and hope to relate in future pages.

King George VI may have had trouble producing his words when faced with a microphone, but the real heroes in that respect were BBC newsreaders dealing with details of Russian towns as our allies in the east took back their territory from the Germans. Regaining places like Dnepropetrovsk and Dneprodzerhinck may have been good news but it was a nightmare to announce. Italian names were easier, although the campaign in that part of Europe was obviously slow and tough. On the other side of the world the Japanese were falling back, island by island, as American troops pushed their way across the Pacific. At home the feeling was that sooner, rather than later, there would have to be a cross Channel landing in Europe.

On a more domestic scale, life at 19 Thicket Road appeared to be heading for trouble when the couple occupying the hall flat moved out. They were a surly and unlikeable pair who apparently told the billeting authorities that their reason for going was "noise made by the children during air raids." The only children occupying the area adjacent to their flat's door at such times were Margaret and I, usually too tired and cold to do anything but wait there with Mum, Nurse Martin, and her dog. Mum told Dad about it one evening when I had gone to bed. I heard him descend the two flights of stairs to the door of the hall flat; the whole house must have heard the way he banged on the door. But the expected confrontation never took place; the flat remained silent. Were our unneighbourly neighbours hiding? I would not have blamed them.

The hall flat's next tenants were a young couple with a baby. The man was an RAF pilot but not the outgoing "wizard prang" type so familiar in film and radio portrayals. He and his family were quiet but friendly and although they only stayed with us a few months I often wonder whether he survived the rest of the war. Each day the news was of RAF night time bombing raids on Germany, while American aircraft played their part during the day. At times they appeared in the sky over north Kent, making the return trip in ragged and incomplete formations tracked by vapour trails. They were usually too high for positive identification, but we felt sure that the four-engined roar could only come from Flying Fortresses. You could look up and feel safe.

German aircraft still came over during the night in what were termed "reprisal" raids for our own constant bombing of cities like Berlin. AA guns round London scored more hits than in 1940-4,1 and among their successes was a Junkers 88 bomber which crashed on the night of February 20 - 21 1944 near the Crystal Palace football ground at Selhurst. That was near enough for me and a couple of other local lads to set off on our bikes, looking for souvenirs. The crash site was well guarded, but a large trailer loaded with salvaged parts gave us the opportunity to help ourselves. My chunk bore a metal label which indicated - in German, of course - that it was something to do with the electrical system. It joined the family collection of blitz relics which already included half of an incendiary bomb extinguished by Dad during his warden duties and some substantial lumps of shrapnel found in the street.

Only a short time later, the night of February 23 - 24, we were once more sheltering in the hallway. Anti-aircraft guns were particularly busy, joined by the occasional - and still frightening - salvo of rockets fired by the Home Guard.

Then we heard a sudden "whoosh!" and explosion with an orange flash visible through the frosted glass of our front doors. "That," said Nurse Martin, "was a bomb." But it did not seem like a bomb. Anything which felt that close would normally have caused more widespread blast damage. We were joined for a second or two by my brother Tony who had been upstairs and realised that it was the house opposite, number 10, which had been hit. As a Civil Defence worker, albeit a junior messenger, he was on his way to see if he could help.

When the All Clear sounded we returned to our warm beds and the full story only became clear the following day. The flash and bang was not caused by a bomb; it was one of the anti-aircraft rockets which had failed to explode in the air and, still a complete missile, nosed its way back to earth. It penetrated the roof of number 10, went through the house and exploded in the basement flat occupied by a middle-aged couple, Mr and Mrs Tom Arnold. Tom survived but his wife, Hilda, died of her injuries the following day.

From our top flat we could look across the road and see the hole in the roof. The only saving grace was that the rocket had not harmed anyone in the other parts of number 10, Mr and Mrs Hughes and their daughters Gwen and Joyce, or Mr and Mrs Rideout in the hall flat. It had, however, wrecked the pride and joy of Mr Hughes - the baby grand piano. It would provide no more Chopin for residents in Thicket Road.

When I remarked to Mum one day that Spring seemed a long time in arriving she told me that one of the first signs she looked out for was in a particular tree across the road, in the front garden of number 12. Directly opposite us was an unchanging fir but to the left was a deciduous specimen with small leaves which, as Mum pointed out, first appeared as a faint green mist among the branches - a hint of better weather approaching. Watching the colour deepen and the leaves thicken was one of the incidental pleasures to come from having a kitchen window high above the street. There were also regular visitors to the window sill, mainly sparrows glad enough to pick up crumbs from the strange grey-brown stuff we called bread. We didn't waste much, but Mum still liked to put any small leftovers out there.

It must have been about this time that we discovered a fault with the electric meter. This was the era of coin-in-the-slot payment for gas and electricity, and we had in one corner of the kitchen a formidable grey gas meter which relied on a constant supply of pennies while the electric meter, only taking shillings, was black, shiny, much smaller and mounted on the wall beneath the window. At regular intervals the meters would be emptied by different men, uniformed and carrying hefty-looking leather bags. They unlocked the cash boxes, spread the money out on the kitchen table, counted it and made notes in a book.

Depending on the amount, there was usually a rebate for the anxious housewife but - and here was the catch - not before weeding out any foreign coins. Most of them were French or Belgian - a hangover from Dunkirk - but other strange denominations appeared as well. Virtually every household had some on standby for those days when, as one wag put it, there was too much week left over at the end of the (legitimate) money.

Now, about our electric meter… At the front of it, on the left and right, were two small silver wingnuts which had been secured by wire seals but for some reason - no names, no pack drill as they used to say - the seals had disappeared. It did not take long to discover that if you undid the wingnuts the front of the meter, complete with the cashbox, could be lifted clear. This opened up all sorts of possibilities, the simplest being to take a shilling from the box, use it to clock up a bob's worth of credit and then put the coin back in the box. Who would know? Another idea was using a piece of folded paper to jam the little wheel that registered how much juice was being consumed but that was topped by Mum's use of the cashbox as an overdraft facility. She kept a mental note of how much it was owed and always made sure that the shillings were paid in before the collector's next visit.

She was at Mrs Shipstone's one morning when the "electric man" arrived at number 13A and emptied the meter there. Mum started to make a discreet exit, thankful that she had enough cash in her purse to top up the meter in our flat.

The man was chatty. “Hang on a minute,” he said. “I’m on my way to your place. I’ll come with you.” Mum played the all-innocence card. “You can’t do that. You’ll have the neighbours talking.” She then fled from 13A, along the road to 19 and upstairs to the flat, dismantled the meter, replaced the money and put the whole thing back together again a couple of minutes before the collector arrived. Mum was always a resourceful woman. All this went on, it need hardly be said, without the knowledge of Dad who seemed to hate parting with any money which did not enhance his social life.

Another little trick developed by Mum involved Dad’s typewriter, his Remington Home Portable, which for many months had apparently been “in hock” at a pawnbroker’s in Gipsy Hill, Upper Norwood. Having spent whatever sum he received for it, Dad was then required to pay interest or lose the machine altogether. When the time came to pay each month, Mum would remind him and Dad would reluctantly part with five shillings or whatever was required. It was always Mum who went to the “pop shop”; Dad would never want to be seen near such places. This suited Mum because, unknown to Dad, she was hiring out the typewriter to the pawnbroker’s son, an arrangement which ensured that she not only kept the interest money but also received a regular payment from the shop owner. Home economics? Mum could have written the book.

Some of 1944’s lengthening daylight time was interrupted by what we termed “nuisance raids” in which

German planes, taking advantage of cloud cover, would drone around while AA guns banged away without any sign of success. The air raid warning kept us all alert but no bombs were heard - just the incessant drone of one aircraft which kept us from going anywhere or doing anything other than waiting. It all seemed pointless, apart from one occasion when the ten-tenths cloud parted and we actually saw the raider. It was heading south and trailing smoke, so we all cheered and waited for the All Clear.

Occasional night time raids continued, heralded by the now-familiar matter of radio programmes losing volume and suffering an echoing kind of interference. The Germans were losing the war, retreating across Russia and gradually giving way in Italy. Hadn't we seen newsreels of their stronghold at Monte Cassino being blown to bits? Why were Jerries bothering with air raids on us?

Into June - and the much-anticipated news that the Allies had landed on the French coast. Normandy? Out came the atlases as fingers pointed to places with names like Caen and Cherbourg and we wondered what a force of 14,000 ships must have looked like, as well as all those planes towing gliders and dropping paratroops. Certain words like Mulberry, Pluto, Juno and Sword took on a new significance and suddenly everybody became an expert on invasion matters and how long the Germans could last out. In the south, Rome had fallen to the Allies - so it was all going well there as well.

Another spell of night time air raids - it must be part of the "Baby Blitz", as they had been dubbed. This was Hitler's last throw of the dice, surely? But suddenly the dice started making a strange noise.

CHAPTER 14 - "SOME SORT OF GLIDER BOMB"

Many people have written about the sound of those pulse-jets we first heard in June 1944. "A motorcycle going uphill...an old Ford Model T car" are among the descriptions. I will add my own version a little later and concentrate instead on the night of Thursday, June 15th when, following a single success two days earlier at Bethnal Green, the Germans launched an estimated 120 of their "Vengeance" weapons, aimed at London.

It must have been the air raid warning that woke us in our top flat. Dad and Tony disappeared to wherever they were needed by the Civil Defence while Mum, Margaret and I got ready to go down and wait in the hall. No need to rush: there was no sound of aircraft or AA guns...but what was that peculiar noise? Inside our unlit lounge, I opened a window and looked towards the south. Over on the left, from the direction of the sound, was a single red light moving steadily towards London. To follow its progress meant nipping to one of the back windows - and there it was, still making that noise, still showing that light and still flying northwards. Eventually eclipsed by the high ground, it could still be heard until the sound stopped abruptly and there was a pause followed by an explosion. So that was it...some sort of weapon - and time for us to leave the flat before another one arrived.

Downstairs, with Nurse Martin and Monty the dog, we waited and wondered about this new development. My verdict: "It's some sort of glider bomb with an engine attached. But why does it show a light?" (Glider bombs, mainly used against shipping, had been in the news). So the Germans had, after all, produced a secret weapon, a topic which cropped up from time to time earlier in the war, but was usually dismissed as "defeatist talk." Then Tony called in, bursting with news. "It's something terrible," he announced. Bless him, he always did like a good panic. Yes, they were flying bombs and there were lots of them. Then he was back on his bike and carrying more messages. We must have gone back to bed at some time but I cannot remember the All Clear. What was the point? This was a new phase; the old rules no longer applied. The following day's newspapers gave the new peril a variety of names.

"Pilotless plane...Buzz bomb...V weapon...P-bomb" were among them, plus "V1" because, it was rumoured, the Germans had other ways of delivering their highly explosive vengeance. Later stories were to give more details, even the proper name "Vergeltungswaffe Eins" with its wingspan of more than 17 feet, and length of 25 feet-plus. The really important parts as far as we were concerned were the one-ton warhead and the crudely pulsating jet engine which produced the noise and red flare while also giving the whole thing a speed of around 350 mph. The name "Doodlebug" cropped up eventually.

In those two or three early days, while the campaign was still new, we became dangerously blasé about these robot bombs. They were being launched from sites in France but always kept to the same routes east of us. The closest we called the number 12 bus route because it appeared to be going via Sydenham; another, slightly further away, we designated number 75 - another bus route.

When a V1 approached we watched confidently from our front windows. "It's all right," Mum would tell people in the street, "this one's on the 12 route." Flippant? Of course it was. These things were still going to fall on other people and we did not know at the time how it would all develop and that it would eventually put the square mile of Penge and Anerley into history.

The awakening came on the afternoon of Sunday, June 18, when we were still, with our false sense of security, watching air activity from the front windows. The doodlebugs appeared to be keeping well to the east, most of them eventually disappearing on their way to London although once or twice we heard the motor cut out, then a pause of a few seconds before the explosion. At this point Dad, through a mixture of night time Civil Defence work and pub-based socialising, had never seen a flying bomb in daylight. He had returned home late in the morning, had lunch and gone for an under-the-eiderdown snooze in the main bedroom, leaving instructions to call him if one of these bombs appeared. It was not long before Mum opened the bedroom door and, raising her voice above the familiar sound of an approaching V1, said, “You’ll get a good view of this one - it’s coming straight towards us.” Dad joined Mum at one of the two windows in the lounge while I watched from the kitchen.

This bomb was flying on a new route; none had been this close before. The noise from its engine was, naturally, louder and had a juddering, penetrating edge. Straight towards us, indeed. The thought crossed my mind: if it cuts out now, we’re in trouble. And that’s what happened.

In the split second before my panic-stricken exit from the kitchen (our windows still had glass in them at this point) I saw the V1 do something unusual - it rolled to its right and flicked over. Why? The question was of little concern to me at the time; I was convinced that the house was about to be destroyed, that there was no escape and that the only thing I could do was keep away from windows and find a doorway which might provide some protection. Trapped on the fourth floor of a collapsing building? Not a hope.

In the lounge, Mum and Dad had taken the emergency a little more calmly. They watched as the flying bomb came down and knew that it would fall short of Thicket Road - then ducked below window sill level. “The flats!” Dad shouted, meaning that Melbourne Court - which lay in the space between Thicket Road and Anerley Park - was about to be hit.

The explosion proved both of us wrong. It was terrifyingly loud, shook the house, smashed the windows and ripped the curtains. As I realised in the dusty aftermath that we were all still alive, Dad hurried past to pick up his Civil Defence gear, get to the bomb site, and help in any rescue work. The V1, one of the first - if not the actual first - to fall in the Penge Urban District, had landed in Anerley Park.

It was, as they say, a pivotal moment. Up to then the whole war experience had been something which happened to other people, almost like a schoolboy game of Cowboys and Indians where someone shouts "Bang! You're dead!" and you fall dramatically, then get up and carry on. Even with a background of genuine sirens, aircraft and explosions - including the near-miss bomb on that winter night in 1940 - I had never been as terrified as in those moments between that V1 starting its dive and then realising I had not been killed.

My age, I suppose, must have had something to do with it, plus a certain amount of good luck. The eight-year-old lad of 1939 had looked forward to the next edition of his favourite comic or the promise of going to the cinema; the 13-year-old of 1944 had grown, had developed deeper feelings, was noticing that girls had interesting shapes and was beginning to look forward to some of the better things that this world - once it sorted itself out - could produce. Of course, any kid at any age wants to grow up but a teenager is starting to have a clearer idea of the future. After all, we were winning the war and good fortune had kept me and the rest of the family from serious harm - but now that could all be wiped out.

There was no more standing in the hall at number 19 for Mum, Margaret and me. Once more we relied on the hospitality of the Shipstones, especially the wonderfully patient Mrs Shipstone whose basement flat was fairly safe from blast damage although what would happen if the upper floors collapsed did not bear too much thought. Number 13A became our second home for the next few weeks. School was out of the question; we had an occasional meal in our top flat just along the road - but always listening out for approaching Doodlebugs. At the first sound we dropped everything and scuttled downstairs, then three doors along. Home was blacked out, anyway. There was no glass in any of the front windows and all we had to keep out the weather was thick, black paper material. Tacked to the window frames it did indeed keep out the weather - but also any sign of daylight. Whenever we were there, electric lights stayed on all the time.

It was the dislodging of this paper when a V1 landed on Trenholme Terrace, about 350 yards away, that provided a sad and uncanny illustration of what blast can do. The bomb hit just before 9.30am on Sunday, July 2nd, and when I went back to the flat, our paper covering on the windows was flapping about and the lounge had a dusty, disturbed look. On the floor were two tightly-folded black, fluffy objects scarcely bigger than the top of a man's thumb. I found a third under the dining table. They had obviously been blown in through the windows - but what were they? A closer look at one of them revealed the tips of tiny ears; they were baby rabbits, gutted and screwed up by the explosion which flung them into our lounge from whichever garden their safe, warm hutch had been standing - as I said, about 350 yards away.

There were human tragedies, too, at Trenholme Terrace. Families died together and there were "if only…" stories of individuals who took one risk too many as the day began. A father, mother and child had spent the night safely in their Anderson shelter but the child wanted one of her favourite toys, which had been left in the house. The father waited until he thought it would be safe and then ventured out. He was still in the house when the V1 struck.

Dad spent most of the day on rescue work at the site. He and other Civil Defence volunteers picked their way through the extensive damage - an exceptional number of houses had been destroyed - looking for the injured but finding too many dead. Their progress was eased by a long garden wall which had been blown flat and provided a ready-made pathway across some of the rubble. Eventually they managed to account for all but one of the residents, a boy. The search continued until the lad's body was found - under the fallen wall. They had been walking over him for most of the day.

When Dad came home he was physically and mentally shattered. Mum asked if it was true that two of

Dad in Civil Defence uniform with his brother Dan, an Army captain. On the right is the Certificate of Thanks issued to all Civil Defence members at the end of the war.

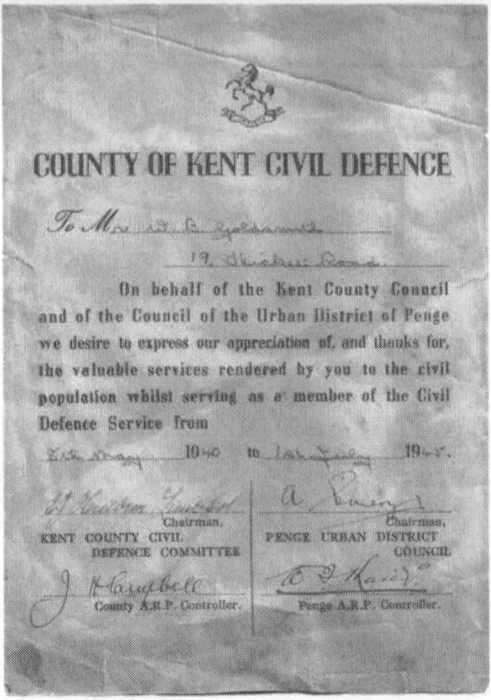

COUNTY OF KENT CIVIL DEFENCE

To Mr [illegible]

[illegible]

On behalf of the Kent County Council and of the Council of the Urban District of Penge we desire to express our appreciation of, and thanks for, the valuable services rendered by you to the civil population whilst serving as a member of the Civil Defence Service from

[illegible] 1940 to [illegible] 194[illegible].

[illegible]
Chairman,
KENT COUNTY CIVIL DEFENCE COMMITTEE

[illegible]
Chairman,
PENGE URBAN DISTRICT COUNCIL

J. Campbell
County A.R.P. Controller.

[illegible]
Penge A.R.P. Controller.

their friends had been killed and he nodded, then broke down and cried.

The number of V1s heading for London was increasing. They came by day and night, sometimes passing in the distance or coming so close that the noise - their own particular penetrating noise - seemed to shake the walls. We had made up beds on the floor of Mrs Shipstone's flat, returning to the arrangements of 1940-41, and could count the flying bombs before eventually falling asleep. Dennis Shipstone and I had made ourselves electric torches, simple arrangements using short pieces of lath wood - plenty of that around from damaged houses - and twin-cell batteries so that we could read in bed. It helped to take our minds off the outside world.

Then we were joined by another family, the Barbers - mentioned elsewhere in these pages - who were apparently related to the Shipstones. They lived in a council house on the corner of Oak Grove and Ash Grove, at Elmers End and I had been to their home on a couple of occasions. They had a son, John, who was near the age of Dennis and me, plus several older offspring. I was never sure of the actual number but when the local council was issuing Anderson shelters to residents in 1940 the Barber family received additional sections. Put together, the whole thing became known as the Blackwall Tunnel and must have done its job because none of them was injured when a V1 fell nearby and the blast rendered their home unsafe. So the Barbers sought temporary respite with the rest of us at 13A Thicket Road - AND started to move in some of their household belongings as well. Where and how was sufficient room found?

A quick reckoning of the numbers. Mrs Shipstone, Dennis and Beryl; Mum, Margaret and me, plus Dad and Tony unless on Civil Defence duty; Mr and Mrs Barber, John and an older girl (Betsy?), plus another daughter who was in the Women's Auxiliary Air Force and was honeymooning with her newly-acquired French-Canadian soldier husband. That makes a maximum of 14 in accommodation which mainly consisted of a kitchen-diner, large front bedroom, large back lounge/reception room and two smaller rooms, all joined by a window-less L-shaped passageway in which we crouched during the day when a V1 went over. At such times we fell into the habit of putting hands over our ears as the house seemed to shake with the penetrating noise from the rackety jet engine. Everyone had the same thought: keeping going! Don't stop! Don't let it be us!

There was a different kind of incident involving a flying bomb when Dennis Shipstone and I were fetching some of the Barber family's household goods, using a builder's two-wheeled cart. Getting the load up the short hill from Elmers End to the Robin Hood crossroads was difficult - but we managed it and continued along Anerley Road, past the library and town hall towards another incline which began by Anerley Park with the garage on our right. Heads down and push - but what was that strange shushing sound with the hint of a whine? We glanced up to see a doodlebug gliding overhead in near-silence. The engine was dead, for whatever reason, but it still had enough air speed to stay aloft although the height was less than a thousand feet. By the time we had realised all this it was too late to do anything other than gape. The bomb continued on its way towards Upper Norwood and then we heard an explosion.

In writing about all this many years later I have tried so far not to include facts and figures that came out afterwards. The intention has been to describe events as they happened and the behaviour of those around us at the time when, perhaps naively, we were wondering how the Germans could still manage to launch so many V1s if Allied aircraft had dropped tons of bombs on the sites in France. And if all the anti-aircraft guns had moved to our south coast, why did they not shoot down most of the doodlebugs? Were the barrage balloons any help - and why didn't RAF fighters shoot down any flying bombs that did get beyond the coast? If Allied troops were in France, how long would it take them to overrun the areas from which the V1s were being launched?

Newspapers and BBC news broadcasts of the time gave some encouragement; yes, the guns and aircraft were stopping many of the V1s and some RAF pilots had developed the art of flying alongside, then using a wingtip to flick the doodlebug over, upsetting its gyroscope control system and making it crash on open countryside. Being pilotless, the bombs took no evasive action and theoretically were sitting ducks when attacked by fighters with gunfire - but an explodiong one-ton warhead demanded some care.

Some of the bombs were exceptionally fast, reaching more than 400mph. While the few early Meteor jets and propellor-driven Typhoons could cope, the Spitfires struggled. At Detling, the fighter station near Maidstone in Kent, some Spitfires were stripped of their camouflage paint and the bare aluminium wings and fuselage polished with Brasso. It gave them an extra 50mph, according to the RAF chap who told me about it many years later. He was a senior man, a God-fearing type who would not have made up the story, and as far as I know this is the first time it has been told in print.

One other discovery I made many years later was that the V1 which terrorised me before it fell in Anerley Park may have been under attack from an RAF fighter. I cannot recall seeing another aircraft at the time - but then my attention was firmly taken by the flying bomb. Its control system might have been hit, which could account for the flick-over movement just before it came down. One other little detail: I found a couple of expended .303 ammunition cartridge cases in the road outside our house immediately afterwards. They had a shiny-new look about them and could not have been there for very long. Did they come from the fighter? It's worth a thought. This was early in the campaign, before the RAF's strategy of intercepting and trying to destroy V1s over open country where there was less chance of causing casualties.

In London and its suburbs the schools may have been empty but adult life carried on with the essential tasks of going to work or shopping. Buses and trains still ran, cinemas were open, the dustmen emptied our bins and Nurse Martin hurried off in her little car, attending to expectant mothers. At the same time everyone had part of their attention diverted, listening out for that sound. What we heard during the Battle of Britain and the blitz had been different. The drone of an aircraft represented something which might drop a bomb - and occasionally did; the harsh, rasping noise of a V1 carried a far more definite threat. It didn't have a crew which wanted to return to base. It was on a one-way trip and would definitely crash and explode on you or somebody else.

CHAPTER 15 - BACK TO THE RICK

It was a relief when Dad told us that Mum, Margaret and I would be going back to Widford in Hertfordshire for another holiday with the Kelly family at The Rick. We arrived to find that there would soon be another Kelly - Miriam was hugely pregnant. There were people in the caravan, including a boy called Brian who was about my age, and we slept in the house. I shared the annexe with Roger, the older boy of Reg and Miriam, settling in quite comfortably and relieved not to keep listening for V1s. They were well to the south of us.

A fortnight passed all too quickly but there was no mention of going back to Anerley. We stayed on, joined for one or two weekends by Dad and even Tony who came for a couple of days and kept us informed of the latest V1 incidents in Penge and Anerley, including the one that fell in Anerley Road shortly after 6pm on Tuesday, July 11.

By his account, Tony had a narrow escape. He left work at 6pm, cycled along Church Road and turned down Anerley Hill when he saw the V1 approaching and wondered whether it would pass overhead. As it started to dive he was still on the upper part of the hill and trying to stop. His bike was a sports machine with dropped handlebars and toe clips on the pedals - all very racy but no good for a quick dismount. Tony claimed that the blast knocked him off the cycle and half way across a gap in the houses left from an HE bomb in 1941. He was shaken but not injured and certainly luckier than other people at the foot of the hill who were waiting for a 654 trolleybus after a day's work at a factory. Along with others, they made a last-minute dash for a nearby shelter but some were among the 17 who died.

Tony also mentioned that the Shipstones had gone to stay with relatives in Stamford, Lincolnshire, where they spent holidays in pre-war days. The basement flat at 13A Thicket Road was left open for use by Tony and Dad as they continued their working lives and still needed a safe place to sleep.

Back in Widford, Mum had come to an arrangement with the Kellys by which, with the new baby due, the three Goldsmiths stayed on at The Rick in return for Mum playing a major part in running the house while I, with my new friend Brian, helped with some of the farm work. Mum mastered the art of cooking on paraffin stoves - even the temperamental Primuses - and we two boys gave a hand with some of the less-skilled work while still managing to have some fun.

Reg Kelly had a favourite quotation about young helpers: "One boy's a boy; two boys is half a boy; and three is no boy at all." Brian and I taught ourselves to converse in backslang, inserting "ag" before every vowel, which meant being able to talk in front of the other children at the farm without giving away any secrets. For errands into nearby places like Hunsdon and Much

Hadham, we acquired a couple of bikes and mine had the novelty of a back-pedal brake. Hunsdon, with RAF Mosquitos still using the airbase, was always an interesting spot although I was shocked by a remark I heard in one of the village shops where the woman proprietor was telling a regular customer about an upset involving the service personnel. It all seemed trivial to me but the woman saw it differently and concluded by remarking, "What do you expect? The RAF take everything and give nothing." This was at a time when the general public already knew the heavy losses of bomber crews who had been attacking Germany. I am still puzzled by the woman's smallminded attitude.

The number of people at The Rick increased by one with the birth of Mrs Kelly's baby. Shame on me, I cannot remember whether it was a boy or girl. Mrs Kelly underwent what was then the statutory post-natal fortnight in bed but her door was always open to visitors, even during breast-feeding time, and she ran the house from the bedroom. In the meantime, while continuing his London-based teaching work, husband Reg found time to drive the tractor which towed the thrasher and binder to start harvesting the farm's corn crop. Brian and I were drafted in to help pick up some of the sheaves and build corn stooks but most of the work was done by a very patient Irish labourer - with the highly unoriginal name of Paddy - who worked at a steady pace and created neat lines.

Reg Kelly surprised me one day by suggesting that he and I build a one-valve radio. He had the parts and the know-how while I had enthusiasm and the patience to do the fiddly bits of wiring under his instruction. With a metal chassis and a faceboard on which to mount the variable condenser, the pair of us had within an hour or two set up a battery-powered receiver capable of getting the two main stations of the time, Home and Forces, to which I listened on headphones. It meant that I could keep closer track of the war news and I remember having a serious discussion with the visiting Tony about the implications of the July 20 bomb plot against Hitler.

Dad continued his weekend visits and brought a series of friends including his tubby fellow air raid warden, Harry Kibble, he of the episode involving a tree which he thought would not have given any shelter from falling shrapnel because it had no leaves. Also seeking temporary relief from the flying bombs was Roland Walbourne, a friend from pre-war days who worked for the Fairey aviation company. He had joined Dad on one of his holidays in Germany and was also involved in their 1938 adventure at Hendon when they flew alongside each other in the rear seats of Hawker Demon bi-plane dive bombers.

The well-spoken Roland had a distinctive voice which suited his inventive sense of humour and the crazy antics it prompted. These were often fuelled by visits to the pub and did not always end well, such as the time he was helping with the harvest and managed to stick a pitchfork in my right thigh.

Most surprising of the visitors was Uncle Dan, my father's younger brother who I had last seen dashing down Anerley Station Road as he returned to India from leave in 1938. An ordinary soldier then, he had by 1944 reached the rank of Captain and was married to Ethel, an Anglo-Indian lady. Their son, Geoff, was at the exploratory age of around two years. For the good-looking and athletic Dan, domestic arrangements in India were several thousand miles to the east and did not stand in the way of his social life in the UK. His easy-going charm worked on the fair sex whether they were in London or out in the wilds of Widford. He was still around when we eventually returned south - but that is for later.

Harvesting work continued with the collection of the dried-out sheaves from their stooks in the field and tossing them up onto a cart drawn by a shire horse on loan from a neighbouring farmer by the name of Topman. The horse was called Major, more for his size than his galloping, and I had the job of leading him in the constant start-and-stop as we crossed and re-crossed the field. Major was not too careful in placing his hooves and I was always glad when, with each full load, the cart went off to be emptied. It gave my feet a chance to recover. The sheaves were stacked and in due course the threshing machine arrived to complete the process that I had seen the year before - the busy, dusty turning of corn sheaves into sacks of grain separated from the chaff and straw. With the benefit of double summertime it went on late into the evening and youngsters were allowed to stay up and watch the harvest home.

Two other vivid memories remain of our time at The Rick which stretched well into September. The first was on Sunday, September 17 when we looked up at dozens of aircraft, many of them towing troop-carrying gliders, obviously on their way to Europe. I made a wild guess that they were going to tackle the Germans in Norway because we seemed to be well established everywhere else. It was, of course, the ill-fated Operation Market Garden which attempted to spearhead a crossing of the Rhine via the bridge at Arnhem. We also looked up again a short while later at returning tug planes, some flying unsteadily and one still dangling its tow rope with what appeared to be part of the glider. The initially up-beat news bulletins gradually toned down over the next few days.

The second memory is of that sound - the rackety roar of a V1 penetrating the annexe and waking everyone in the early hours. "It's a P-bomb!" said Roger Kelly, who shared the room. In that normally quiet rural setting - and not having heard one for several weeks - it did not seem possible; but there it was, getting louder and approaching from a northerly direction. Through the uncurtained windows we saw it, flying low and with the familiar red glare from its jet engine as it passed from left to right and continued towards London with the light gradually disappearing and the noise losing its guttural edge until it disappeared completely. We never heard an explosion, so it must have come down many miles further away.

That, thankfully, was my last doodlebug and it must have been launched from an aircraft. Most of the ramps in France which had kept up such a steady flow of V1s in the mid-summer weeks were by the middle of September being overrun by Allied troops or bombed out of existence. The comparatively few missiles air-launched at night were still deadly but the main onslaught was over; we could breathe again - or so we dared to think.

Dad must have considered that it was safe enough for Mum, Margaret and me to leave Widford and return to Anerley. We said farewell to the Kelly family and headed south, with my luggage including the one-valve radio which I was sure would astonish my friends. In fact, despite my best efforts, it never worked again. Back in south London it was a case of noting the new gaps in streets, finding out who else had returned from extended holidays and discovering what arrangements could be made for resuming school. The formidable Oakfield was still there but senior boys had to be accommodated at the similarly Victorian building in Melvin Road, sharing it with senior girls.

Other families who had sought temporary refuge from the V1s by moving outside London appeared to be in no hurry for the return journey. This was an unexpected benefit for those who did resume school. I was placed in the 3A class, taught by Mr Warren, and as one of only 16 pupils was able to do more than just make up for lost time. Smaller classes did indeed produce better work for the few weeks before larger numbers made it necessary for all senior boys to return to Oakfield.

Among those who reappeared were the Shipstones, back from Stamford where Dennis had actually worked at a factory producing fenders for small ships. Ian Robinson, from number 8, also turned up having returned from official evacuation to Huddersfield. He told colourful stories of having to help with the potato harvest and being among a gang of boys from his school who were urged to “pick oop them tayties, lads. ’Eds down an’ arses oop.” Incidentally, it was Ian’s step-father who, on leave from the army earlier on in the V1 campaign, allegedly decided to go back early because he couldn’t stand the constant danger.

ABOVE: Wardens of the Civil Defence in a march-past during one of the National Savings weeks in Penge.
BELOW: The formidable and now long gone senior school for boys in Oakfield Road, Penge.

CHAPTER 16 - WHAT IF...?

Perhaps this is the point at which I can break out of the narrative as something being written in a what-we-knew-at-the-time style and throw in a spot of reflection, coupled with statistics since quoted in various publications. I refer mainly to the V1 campaign which, had it been launched earlier, could have proved a far deadlier setback in terms of fatalities, injuries, and destruction among people and their ways of life in London and its suburbs.

To the Urban District of Penge, the last acres of Kent nudging up against Croydon and Lambeth at the top of Anerley Hill, fell the dubious distinction of receiving the most V1s on a per-acre basis. Three of them fell in the grounds of the Crystal Palace where they did little damage but the others killed more than 80 people. Compare that with the figure of 104 enemy action deaths in Penge for the whole war. Of the hundreds of flying bombs launched against London, many were stopped short by the reorganised lines of defence - barrage balloons, anti-aircraft guns and RAF fighters. I have since read the claim that the RAF brought down 1,999 of 9,000 launched; AA guns, once they received ammunition with proximity fuses, also claimed hundreds; and balloons, grouped to provide a curtain of steel cables, were far more effective that they had ever been when scattered among London parks during the blitz of 1940-41. The "what if…?" game is dangerously addictive when it comes to imagining what could have happened, compared with how events actually turned out. For example, would Germany's invasion of Russia have succeeded if the campaign had started five weeks earlier - as was originally planned - instead of being held up by the need to help when Italy's attack on Greece went wrong? Nearer home, what would have happened if V1s and V2s had been ready to launch six or even twelve months earlier than the time at which they actually started arriving?

One other fact which may be a surprise - the city which received the most V1s and V2s was not London; it was Antwerp. It became "the city of sudden death" as the retreating Germans threw everything at the port which would serve as the main landing point for supplies needed to maintain the Allied advance.

Now back to the family and other events.

CHAPTER 17 - THE LAST WARTIME CHRISTMAS

There is a photograph of Dad, Uncles Dan and Jim and brother Tony, taken in the latter part of 1944 by one of the Streatham News Series photographers, Peter Eastment. Their smiles are probably alcohol-assisted (Tony would have been 18 about this time) and Peter was with them in a purely social capacity. Dad, for once, is not wearing his Civil Defence uniform and Dan is in "mufti" - not an expression used these days - with no sign of his Army rank of captain. Just as well, because Jim has his forage cap at a jaunty angle and is wearing a uniform which indicates that three or four years of service life has not changed him. He is still scruffy; he is still a private. Tony has all the confidence of a teenager and will, within a year or so, also be in the Army.

Dan was on a long leave from India and had collected a succession of lady friends some of whom, even after he had gone back east, continued to call in on our family at Thicket Road. One of them had what was referred to as a "bump" which makes me wonder how many other cousins Margaret, Tony, and I have. Another of these close friends was Dorrie, part of the weekend drinking school whose husband was somewhere abroad with the Army. I had met Dorrie a few months earlier when at a fun fair at a park somewhere in Norwood. Having already spent my money on some of the more inexpensive amusements, I was rescued by the surprise arrival of Mum, Dad, and some of their pub friends including Dorrie who took me several times on the racing car circuit, one of the more pricey novelties, and insisted on my driving.

By the next time I saw her, Dan was on the scene and they had become an item.

They had heard that I was keen on seeing the film "Fantasia", then showing at Studio One near Oxford Circus, and promised to take me. Dorrie explained that the Disney attraction was mainly cartoon interpretations of classical music and said we could go to any other film as long as it was not about the war. I already knew about the classical music and had developed a liking for it ever since school days at St Sidwell's in Exeter where listening to a radio programme on orchestral works was part of the curriculum. Seeing what Disney would do to illustrate part of Beethoven's Pastoral Symphony or Tchaikovsky's Dance of the Sugar Plum Fairy was an interesting prospect - and Mickey Mouse would be having magical trouble, too.

So, one afternoon the three of us went by bus to the Tottenham Court Road end of Oxford Street and strolled towards Oxford Circus - a walk I would take many times much later in life when going to work for an ITV company. In 1944 London was still a novelty for me with so many people in every kind of uniform packing its pavements. At Studio One we saw "Fantasia" plus "Hotel Du Nord", an enjoyable romance with French sub-titles, but the Disney film was one of the best I had ever seen, full of imagination and humour with the colourful graphics interspersed by some amusing live sequences with the narrator and orchestra.

We emerged into a blacked-out world, crossed carefully to the north side of Oxford Street, and linked arms for the walk back to Tottenham Court Road, singing "Roll Me Over in the Clover" and feeling with our feet for kerbstones at the junctions with Wells Street, Berners Street, and others. The bus for Crystal Palace made it an easy journey back, and at the start I managed to grab the seat next to Dorrie. We were upstairs and when somebody vacated the front seat Dan said, "Let's move forward." I fell for the trick, hurried to the front, and Dan moved into where I had been sitting. Fair enough - at least he had paid for the cinema and the bus fares.

It was also about this time that Dad, anticipating my starting work in just over a year, began to teach me shorthand. There were no evening classes at the time and having taken me through the basic straight strokes - pee, bee, tee, dee, chay, jay, kay, gay - he bought a Pitman's primer and let me get on with it. The first chapter only repeated those first strokes; the rest - iff, vee, ifth, thee and everything else - followed in an increasingly bewildering series of chapters which completely defeated me. I had made the mistake of sneaking a look at the final page and seeing an exercise which encompassed every feature of shorthand including positional writing, grammalogues, large and small circles, the halving principle, ell-hooks and arr-hooks. I was not a good pupil and gave up but then resumed with a new determination to take it at a slow and steady pace.

Dad, by contrast, had always been able to learn quickly and did not seem to understand anyone - particularly his younger son - who could not cotton on immediately to anything which related to language and writing. He didn't mean it, but I found his presence and attitude intimidating. It affected me badly when, having learned enough shorthand to attempt something outside the basic sphere of "Dear Sir, We are in receipt of your esteemed order…", I was given the task of taking down the BBC news at dictation speed. In the latter part of the war this was featured at the end of normal bulletins in the mornings and meant for listeners in service units abroad who produced their own newspapers.

The dictation was slow enough to be taken down by a competent typist but for the shorthand learner who needed time to conjure up a readable outline for "Eindhoven" or "Dusseldorf" or some of the military terms it was a nightmare. My hand used to shake and, as I fell behind, the outlines became more and more illegible. I can remember one bulletin which opened with "Hanover and Essen have fallen…" and being grateful that they were two places I could easily transcribe when it came to sorting out my notes. In later life I would meet official recorders for whom the spoken word went from ear to hand - that is, they did not have to think about it - and although my speed did improve I was never in that league.

Early in September 1944, it appeared that the Germans had yet another secret weapon, the V2 rocket. None of these fell in the Urban District of Penge but they were certainly heard. As one radio commentator said some time later, "When you hear the explosion, you are convinced that it has fallen in the next street no matter how far away it has landed." It certainly was a loud noise which I heard on several occasions followed, of course, by the whooshing sound of its arrival. That was the uncanny point of being attacked with a supersonic weapon - you couldn't hear it coming; there were no air raid warnings and, given that its speed on arrival was around 2,500mph, only a few people ever claimed to have seen one.

Official news sources had been slow to acknowledge the use of V2s but there was no hiding the fact that 286 shoppers and staff died when one fell on Woolworth's at New Cross, south London, during the busy Saturday of November 25. I don't recall any shock or outrage at the time, indeed my main impression is of our form master at Oakfield School, Mr A.H. Warren, being told about it the following week by one of the boys, looking incredulous and asking, "You mean it actually landed on the store?" No such thing as saturation news coverage in those days; it was all "too sensitive" for the blue pencil brigade.

Penge had four near-misses from the rockets early in 1945 - two to the north in Sydenham at Crystal Palace Park Road (nine killed) and Wells Park and two to the south in Cator Park and Lennard Road, Beckenham. No casualties from those last three.

On the near-Continent the Allies had been making steady progress, apart from a sudden reversal in December at what later became known as the Battle of the Bulge just as we at home were preparing for another austerity Christmas while hoping that it would really prove to be the last of the war. In 1994 I wrote about it in a Christmas edition of the Adscene series of newspapers, based in Canterbury and covering most of Kent. The article was headed: "They couldn't ration the laughs" and has been retrieved from my archives…

"Fifty years ago we celebrated what was to be the last Christmas of the Second World War.

"It was not to be the last as far as food rationing was concerned but it did mark the end of a year which had included a mini-blitz, the V1 and V2 weapons, the Allied landings in Normandy and a feeling that the wartime show had moved on. The front line was in Europe, not at the Channel coast.

"Several weeks earlier, around November, the first preparations towards Christmas dinner began when my mother made three puddings. Two were for us; the third was for a neighbour. We all knew what ought to go into a Christmas pudding. One of my mother's more unusual pastimes was to read aloud extracts from a Mrs Beeton recipe book we had found when we moved into our flat in Anerley.

“Those which began with such phrases as ‘Take a dozen eggs, three pints of cream and the flesh of four chickens’ were guaranteed to reduce us all to hysterical laughter. Our egg ration was one per person per month, cream was unheard of and the last time I had seen four chickens was in my grandmother’s backyard in Sussex before the war. The more outlandish the ingredients required by Mrs Beeton, Victorian mistress of good housekeeping, the louder the laughter. At ‘Take four pounds of the best steak…’ we chuckled; at ‘Half a dozen roasting fowls…’ we howled; for ‘Half a dozen fresh lemons, a dozen oranges and a dozen bananas…’ we roared.

“I don’t remember the exact recipe for those wartime Christmas puddings but they included some flour, breadcrumbs, as much dried fruit as our ration points would allow, black treacle, grated carrot and - to help the darkening process - a quantity of draught Burton beer from the bottle and jug bar at the Thicket Hotel. The wonderful mixture was placed into pudding basins, topped with greaseproof paper and tied off with pudding cloths. Then they were cooked and stored. At about that time, in thousands of other kitchens, other mothers were weaving their own culinary magic.

“It would be the same story when Christmas morning arrived and, with the puddings already being steamed, there came the task of preparing dinner itself.

There was no shortage of ideas from well-meaning people at the Ministry of Food. Earlier in the war they had produced a recipe for something called Woolton Pie - named after Lord Woolton, the Minister of Food. It consisted entirely of vegetables in a pie crust and I have never met anyone who actually remembers tasting it. The idea alone was enough to give a hungry man what the wonderful Daily Mirror columnist Cassandra once described as 'the dry heaves.'

"But the dear old Ministry had a willing ally in the BBC whose Home Service used to put out a programme called The Kitchen Front introduced by Freddy Grisewood. This, too, would trot out recipes and all sorts of ideas from women whose 'refained' accents never belonged in a kitchen and made them the object of scorn. What was the point of trilling on about Mock Goose, Mock Duck or Mock Oyster when most of us didn't know what the real stuff tasted like, anyway? 'Mock off!' said mother as she switched over to the Forces programme.

"In the really dark days of the early 1940s, the greatest resource in feeding the nation was the sheer determination and ingenuity of the average housewife. Having worked wonders when the U-boats were winning the Battle of the Atlantic, they were able to create worthy Christmas dinners when less troubled convoys brought in extra food. Cargoes not destined for the shops were for the American forces and since everyone seemed to know somebody who knew somebody else with access to these supplies, a lot of GI goods found their way into British homes. Washington must have been puzzled; according to their calculations, the average American serviceman smoked 200 cigarettes a day and weighed 30 stone.

"Our extra in 1944 was a turkey, won by my brother in a raffle at work. It wasn't particularly big; its demise must have been a photo-finish between the guy who wrung its neck and anorexia. But it was a turkey. Other meat was more generally available for that Christmas than the previous two or three years. Even the novelty of Spam, supplied by our American cousins, was beginning to wear off.

"So the Christmas dinner would not have been frugal or make-believe. The vegetables, even accompanied by tinned peas, may have tasted all the better for being part of the produce from Dad's 'Dig for Victory' allotment. Dad, back from the pub at some time after two o'clock and arriving full of beer and benevolence, completed the family of five. As we ate, the radio took us around the Commonwealth, to places healthily pink in the school atlas. The mood was even more optimistic than usual; we were all part of a winning team.

"By the time the last of the Christmas pudding had been scraped from the plates, the radio tour had returned to London and the King. George VI, whose elder daughter turned 18 that year, was never at ease with the microphone. With millions of others we hung on his words, tense with the effort of willing him through the interminable pauses and pain of articulation. But everyone listened, even if it was to be endured rather than enjoyed.

"At a few minutes past three, with the national anthem safely out of the way, we all relaxed again and studied for the umpteenth time the programmes promised in the ornate double-page spread of the Radio Times for Monday, December 25, 1944. By the same time in 1945 the war would be over, although ration books were to remain until July 1954. But in the afterglow of skinny turkey and miraculous pudding we felt secure. Well-fed ignorance really was bliss."

Footnotes to the article:

1: Adscene readers enjoyed it, and I even received a phone call from someone who had also bought Burton beer from the Thicket Hotel's bottle and jug. The pub, on the right-hand side as you travel towards Anerley hill, has been converted into flats.

2: "Daily Mirror" columnist Cassandra - real name William Connor - coined that phrase "the dry heaves" in connection with some topic other than Woolton Pie, during his post-war writing. Already famous for his acerbic comments on national and international matters, he went into the army during the war and served overseas. On his return, he opened his first column with the words, "As I was saying when I was so rudely interrupted…"

CHAPTER 18 - HELL ON EARTH

To add a postscript about 1944, it was the year in which I wore my first pair of long trousers and then celebrated my 14th birthday on December 9th. On the last day of term at Oakfield I stood in the back row at morning assembly and sang "The Day Thou Gavest, Lord, is Ended" although, unlike most of the other boys of my age, I would not be leaving school then. Among those who did leave were Dennis Shipstone and Len Quinnell, each carrying an envelope with a generously-worded reference from Mr Margham, the headmaster.

With no father on hand to provide help or advice about his future, Dennis had asked my father if he knew of any worthwhile jobs for a beginner - and had been referred to Samuel Stephens Ltd, the company which housed and printed the Streatham News Series of local papers as well as printing a variety of other large-circulation work including national magazines. It was the building in Belvedere Road, Upper Norwood, where Dad worked as assistant editor and was respected among the works staff. Dennis must have made the right impression when he was interviewed because he was taken on as a junior and, after the usual few odd-job months began - and eventually completed - an apprenticeship in the warehousing side of the print business. Len Quinnell began with Penge Urban District Council, working with those on the considerable task of rebuilding its war-damaged housing stock.

At school, with little or no central heating in our large, high-ceiling class, the winter temperature had us all shivering - but there was an old-fashioned stove which gave our teacher, Mr Warren, the idea of sending out some of the boys to go and find firewood from nearby bomb sites. They returned with enough fuel to get the stove going and take the edge off the chill although the idea was dropped after a few days. Mr Warren was beginning to suspect that not all the wood came from bomb sites and that nearby houses, undamaged so far, were starting to lose chunks of garden fences.

In any case, I was spending less time in the classroom because the headmaster kept "borrowing" me to take on small tasks - like reorganising the stock room and listing the various text-books, many of which were out of date. It was during this job that I came across a single multi-coloured chart for teaching touchtyping. Mr Margham said I could have it, so I took it home and showed Dad who had only ever used two fingers on each hand to hammer out his 35,000-word Woolworth's Sixpenny Library detective and romance stories. His own Remington Home Portable machine was not available - probably on one of its visits to the pawnbroker - but he said I could use the office typewriter at the radio receiving station the next time I delivered his sandwiches.

That was the start of proper typing instead of the "hunt and peck" method during my previous limited experience. I went through the exercises (A-S-D-F-G-F etc) and found, like many other beginners, that my little finger on each hand was at first barely strong enough to use the keys. I even had a go on a teleprinter and had to get used to the "figs and caps" method necessary for a machine with only three banks of keys. Dad would soon be edging me even closer to the working world but in the meantime the war news continued and, as we moved further into 1945, places captured by the Russians were sounding less eastern and more German.

A lot happened in April, including the sudden death of American President Roosevelt who had, only a few weeks earlier, been seen in newspapers and on newsreels with our own Winston Churchill and Russian leader Joseph Stalin at Yalta on the Black Sea. It was a meeting to make decisions about the shape of the post-war world. Roosevelt died on the 12th; on the 15th millions gasped as Allied troops in the west entered Belsen, the German concentration camp which revealed hellish scenes.

It was among the first but by no means the worst of the camps to be uncovered; nevertheless, the hundreds of skeletal bodies, stacked in heaps and flung into huge, half-filled pits, were the stuff of nightmares. And yet some were still alive, striped rags covering emaciated frames as they tottered among the evidence of deliberate death on an industrial scale. BBC commentator Richard Dimbleby fought to keep the emotion from his voice as he brought the news to listeners while the newspaper pictures left most readers stunned.

At the cinema a few days later the programme was stopped before the newsreel and the lights came on while staff members in the aisles warned that film of the concentration camp was about to be shown. Those who could not face it were allowed to wait in the foyer until the newsreel was over and then resume their seats. Most people stayed. At times in the preceding years they may have wondered about the reason for the war; now they knew.

CHAPTER 19 - VE AND VOTING

The last few days of April added to the news. By the 25th, Berlin had been surrounded by the Russians and two days later the BBC afternoon news announced "East and West have met" - the Allies and Russians had finally come together in a meeting which, as filmed for the newsreels, was a great show of comradeship, the usual swapping of hats and attempts to communicate. On the 28th Benito Mussolini and his mistress Clara Petacci perished at the hands of Italian partisans, but the biggest cheer was on the 30th when news filtered through that Hitler was dead.

There had been a song a couple of years before - "When that man is dead and gone...we'll go dancing down the street, kissing everyone we meet..." but I don't think many - if any - did that. The general feeling was of relief, plus grim smiles that a long-awaited comeuppance had been delivered; grisly details would follow.

By the beginning of May, the war had only a few days to run - and we knew it. I could remember the teacher in 1A at Oakfield, Mr Letch, talking about the end of the First World War and assuring us that it had not come as a surprise - "We knew it was going to end that day" - which seemed strange, thinking back to 1942 when our teacher used to rave at idle boys - "Sailors risking their lives to bring you food!" - at the height of the Battle of the Atlantic. Now the enemy leaders were dead and armies in Germany, Italy, Holland and Denmark were surrendering.

To add a thoughtful note: it was less than six weeks since the last British civilian had been killed by enemy action - a V2 rocket which fell at Orpington on March 27th.

Early in the afternoon of Monday, May 7th, I was with a bunch of friends in that stretch of Thicket Road between numbers 13 and 19. Gwen Hughes, Dennis and Beryl Shipstone were there because it was our usual meeting place - there was little or no traffic and virtually no parked cars at that time. There was a sense of anticipation because one or two flags had already appeared at windows. Our general chatter - teenagers are never short of something to talk about - was interrupted by a woman opening a window and calling out, "The war is really over!" She had just heard a radio announcement about Germans signing the unconditional surrender.

That was the cue for more flags and decorations to appear. Even people who usually kept a low profile were putting up bits of bunting and, as each little display was completed, we moved from house to house and cheered their efforts. Then we all went indoors to join our families and have the first peacetime tea since September 1939. Later, when Dad came home, we were back in the street and linking arms with Mr White the milkman and his wife from number 8, plus others including Nurse Martin - I think - to sing "Blaze Away" ("We'll make a bonfire of our troubles…") as well headed up to Anerley Road and along to the shops near the junction with Hamlet Road where a crowd had gathered and a bonfire really was blazing away.

The following day was declared VE Day - Victory in Europe, because British troops of the 14th Army in Burma and American forces in the Pacific were still fighting the Japanese. To me, having an official VE Day seemed a bit false because impromptu celebrations are usually the best. That is why my abiding memory of that time is the way we - Beryl, Dennis, Gwen and I - went from house to house, applauding those first flags.

Our own official celebrations the following day included a bonfire in Thicket Road to burn effigies of Hitler and Goering. We were joined by the father of a boy, Kenneth Stebbings, who lived at number 12 and had just been released from the army following service in North Africa. We wanted to know if he had killed any Germans and he said, “Yes, one.” He added, “When I searched his body I found that he had letters and photographs from his home. I don’t suppose he wanted to be there any more than I did, so I didn’t kill anyone else.”

Downstairs neighbour Nurse Martin was keen to see the crowds in London and so we - Mum, Margaret and I - went with her on May 9th, the evening after the official celebration when there were still thousands of people milling around Piccadilly, Trafalgar Square, The Mall and Buckingham Palace. They, too, had come “to see the crowds” which even then struck me as strange. The other people in the crowds had come to see us just as much as we had come to see them - so who formed the crowd?

My main memory of that occasion is trying to keep with the other three in Trafalgar Square and then moving into The Mall. At the far end, behind Buckingham Palace, two searchlights stabbed a huge "V" into the night sky. Getting through Admiralty Arch was scary; only the two narrow side passages were open and being caught in the crush edging forward felt like an invitation to disaster. There was a strange silence; people with arms pressed to their sides and moving half a step at a time frowned warnings at each other: "Stay upright! Don't trip! Keep calm!" It was a strange way to enjoy yourself.

Also around this time, I had noticed that Winston Churchill's appearance on a cinema newsreel was met with near-silence. Up to a few months beforehand he was being applauded as the man who had seen us through the dark days when we stood alone against an enemy who had conquered most of Europe. There had been an afternoon a year or so earlier when Mum, Margaret and I had stood on Anerley Road with many other people waiting to see Churchill pass by in an open car, as part of a visit to the area. We were rewarded with a close-up of the man, his cigar and V-sign and we all clapped and cheered. Now the applause had gone and when I asked Dad why this was happening, he exploded, "Because Churchill is the leader of the Tory party!" I said, "Oh," or something equally non-committal because when Dad spoke like that it was clear that he expected you to know all about the subject.

Why didn't someone take me - and quite a few others - on one side and say something like, "Look, there's this strange thing called politics."? They could have added, "Politics have always been around - it's just that during the last five and a half years our leaders have, in the main, put their political differences aside and got on with the job of winning the war in Europe. Thanks to them and a bit of help from the rest of the world, that has been achieved but now the different groups want a General Election so that one of them forms a Government and the other becomes the Opposition and they can sit in the House of Commons and shout at each other."

As most young people understood it, Labour stood for progress and Conservative for keeping things the same, while nobody was sure what the Liberals wanted. The few Communists were tolerated in view of the wartime Alliance with Russia. They called each other "comrade" and tended to wear scruffy roll-neck jumpers. In what seemed to be indecent haste, a General Election was called for July 5th - at a time when British troops were still fighting the Japanese in the Far East. Proxy votes were arranged for our boys in the forces - but it didn't feel right. Those in Burma were regarding themselves as "the Forgotten Army."

I was puzzled by the first political posters which carried pictures of familiar leader Winston Churchill and Anthony Eden, his Foreign Secretary since 1942. The slogan was "Vote National" - no mention of Conservative. There was no confusion about parties at a local level - Edward Campbell was the Conservative, Alexander Bain stood for Labour and the uniformed figure of Major Jasper

Sayer smiled down as the Liberal. Anyone who represented Penge would be a Labour man, I assumed, but Mum warned that we were also tied in with the much more Conservative areas of Beckenham and Bromley.

Even in Penge and Anerley there would be Conservative voters - "Like Doris from the Paragon" added Mum. Doris - she must have had a surname - ran an ironmonger's shop, Paragon Supply, in Anerley Road and sold everything from dustbins to fuse wire in addition to dishing out gallons of paraffin, the smell of which never left her. I suppose Mum was making the point that someone who ran a successful business would not want to see too many changes - but for a long time I associated paraffin with Conservatism. And this was long before Esso Blue.

One evening Dad, Mum and I went to an election meeting for the Liberal man, Major Jasper Sayer, who appeared in an ordinary suit because while candidates could be pictured in uniform they were not allowed to wear it while addressing a political meeting. There were two other speakers but none of them made much impression on me apart from the way they stressed that while Winston Churchill was a great leader, the rest of the Conservatives did not add up to much. They said it was like the local grocer saying that you could have a tin of salmon as long as you also bought half a dozen tins of Spam.

Jasper Sayer must have said something that impressed Dad, who voted for him. So did 12,176 other people, while Bain polled 19,849 and Campbell won with 26,108. It was a short-lived triumph; he died on July 17th and at a by-election four months later the Conservatives parachuted in Harold Macmillan, formerly at Stockton-on-Tees, one of the many "safe" Tory seats overrun in July's Labour landslide of 393 successes. Dad saw this as an opportunity to have a tilt at one of the old-established ruling families and switched his alliance from Sayer to Bain. It made no difference; Macmillan increased the Conservative vote and began a long tenure as MP for Bromley, Beckenham, and Penge.

It is worth recording that a year or two later, when Dad became an Independent member of Penge Urban District Council, he chaired one of Macmillan's regular and largely non-political "Month in Parliament" meetings at Anerley Town Hall. The MP agreed with the way that Dad, in his introduction, stressed the informative and non-party nature of the event and - while it didn't change Dad's overall views - he became something of a Macmillan fan and treasured the friendly letter of thanks he received from the MP. The letter, incidentally, is held by my sister Margaret - pressed in the pages of a copy of "The Middle Way."

Time to rewind to the early summer of 1945 just after VE Day and the family's renewed connection with Eastbourne. It began with a day trip when Tony went down by train and later reported that the seafront was stripped of anti-invasion material and getting back to being an essential part of the resort. I think he managed to see Aunt Rose and her son Geoff, back from their wartime stay in Gloucestershire and waiting for Uncle Tom's demobilisation from the Army. Tony had always been a favourite with Rose and Tom, going back to the time when - long before I arrived on the scene - they used to take him out in his pram whenever Mum, Dad and their new son were in Eastbourne.

It must have been a few weeks later that I persuaded Mum to let me visit the town with Dennis Shipstone. I wrote to Uncle Bill and Aunt Mona who still lived at 62 Bexhill Road - an address full of memories for the whole family - and they replied that Dennis and I would be welcome for a weekend. Armed with some food essentials for our hosts, we were taken by Mum to East Croydon station on a Friday afternoon and seen onto the train. It was my first journey to the coast since 1939 and Dennis had never been to Eastbourne before so I was able to point out some of the landmarks that Tony and I had always anticipated on our annual trips to stay with Gran. The two most familiar were on the South Downs: the "V" - for Queen Victoria, we were always told - formed by trees and the Long Man of Wilmington whose chalky outline meant that we were almost there.

The familiar blue and yellow Eastbourne Corporation buses had not disappeared and we headed for the Archery, the pub at the foot of Channel View Road which led to Bexhill Road where the last but one was number 62. Uncle Bill and Aunt Mona had hardly changed but Molly had become a schoolgirl and there were two newcomers, non-identical twins Rita and Mary. I introduced Dennis and we were made welcome with a cup of tea while swapping family news. George Farrant, he of the "I can't see no blasted swaddikas" episode in 1940, was no longer there. I think he had moved to be with a daughter near London, found a part-time job, and then died following an appendicitis operation.

Uncle Bill - as we called him - was George Farrant's son by a failed marriage and not a blood relation to the Arnolds, my mother's family. Before the First World War, Bill had moved into number 62, with his sister Lil, when his father joined the widowed Margaret Arnold plus her bunch of two sons and three daughters. Then the "miracle" Katherine arrived, later calling herself Rose. Ten in a modest three-bedroom terraced house; where did they all sleep?

But everybody liked Uncle Bill; he took the simple approach to life, had a great sense of humour and was devoted to his wife and family in addition to being a lifelong servant of the Eastbourne Waterworks Company. His favourite work story concerned the time when, as a turncock, he was called out of bed in the early hours to deal with a burst main outside the Town Hall. This involved inserting a large key, topped by a substantial iron ring, into a hydrant in the middle of the road. One end of a four-foot metal bar was inserted through the ring and the rest used as a lever with Bill walking in a circle in order to close off the flow of water. He was wet, cold and fed up; the only witness was a latenight reveller who asked: "Wotcher doin', mate?" Bill pointed up at the illuminated face of the municipal timepiece and replied, "I'm winding up the ….ing clock!"

On the late Friday afternoon of our visit there was enough time for Dennis and me to dash to the southern end of Channel View Road for a reunion with the sea. The thrill was still the same; a few strides across rough ground until the shingle gradually forced us into a crunching, stone-scattering climb to the point where a mid-tide view of the English Channel presented itself, grey-green, shifting, breaking and breathing in our faces. We waved at it; we threw stones at it; we even tasted it - yes that was the sea. To our right, the pier looked in need of a wash and brush-up and there was no sign of the "Glen Gower" paddle steamer which used to ply between Eastbourne and Hastings. But we inhaled a mixture of ozone and optimism, turned and made our way to Princes Park to check on the substantial 18-hole pitch-and-putt course as well as the yachting pond.

Saturday's weather could have been better but we just had to go swimming at least once before venturing west along the full length of the promenade and onto the steeply rising ground which eventually led to Beachy Head and the view down over the lighthouse. Sunday was even better; bright sunshine tempted us to more crowded beaches between the pier and the bandstand where there were girls - girls in bathing costumes to make 14-year-old boys start thinking about life beyond Biggles books and cowboy films. We swam in the sea and then sunbathed on our backs, swam again and sunbathed on our fronts, then repeated the process until both of us began to feel rather pink. Then it was time for tea at Bexhill Road and sincere thanks to Uncle Bill and Aunt Mona, plus all the promises to pass on their best wishes to Mum, Dad and the rest of the family. It had been a weekend, part-nostalgic, part-exploratory but wholly unsupervised, that neither Dennis nor I would ever forget.

CHAPTER 20 - TWO BIG BANGS

It could have been only a few weeks later that most of the family went to Eastbourne for a couple of weeks. Tony, now 19 and with his own social life, stayed in Anerley. For some reason - perhaps it was cheaper than the train - Mum, Margaret and I travelled down by bus to East Grinstead, changed to the Southdown service as far as Hailsham and then took the steam train to Hampden Park. Our parents stayed with the Hall family while Margaret and I were with a next-door neighbour - their name was Hagger or Haiger - and I was the first occupant of a bedroom kept for their son who had been a prisoner of war in Japanese hands. The tragic story was that while being transferred from one camp to another by sea, his boat had been sunk by the Allies. All his parents ever saw again were the tattered remains of his last postcard to them.

The big difference about staying at Hampden Park was not being able to pop along the road to visit the beach. That was now a once-a-day treat because it took train or bus fares and, as usual, we were short of money although Dad didn't appear to cut down on his pub visits. One memorable moment on the first or second day of our arrival: the four of us were walking up the last few yards of Terminus Road before it met the seafront and Dad looked at me, then at Margaret and put a finger to his lips.

We looked at the expression on her face as, for the first time in her eight years, an encouragingly blue English Channel came into view. "Is that the sea?" she asked.

We crossed to the promenade, turned right and passed the bandstand on our way towards the Wish Tower where Aunt Vi - married to Mum's brother Charles - was in charge of the ice cream stand. Margaret was given some money and told to ask for an ice cream, then say, "Thank you, Auntie Vi", by way of a surprise reintroduction after the wartime gap. It didn't work; Vi saw a little girl arriving and just said, "Sorry - sold out" - which left Margaret stranded. Then Vi recognised Mum and Dad. We still didn't get any ice cream that day but were all right for the rest of our holiday.

Only one flavour was available, served in no-nonsense blobs, as the ice cream business and everything else recovered the holiday mood during rationing and the inevitable shortages. There was no lack of people trying to make money in the candid snapshot business. Young men combed the beaches and promenade, carrying their cameras - "How about a group with the family?" - and wearing red berets. Many were, indeed, newly-demobbed servicemen but not all of them had been in the Parachute Regiment - it was just a way of trying to cash in on the sympathy still felt for those so badly mauled during the Arnhem disaster.

We caught a westbound bus, got off at the top of East Dean Road and walked along the top of the South Downs towards Willingdon, looking down on Eastbourne to our right, still noticeably detached from Hampden Park and with the amusing distant spectacle of trains travelling between the two stations appearing to merge with each other, shorten, stretch and then separate like some worm-like creature. Every point along the Downs seemed to have its own name - Crow Crouch and the Beehive among them - recalled by Dad from his own youthful time as one of the many Goldsmiths in that part of the world. Not there at the time of our walk, but discovered in later years, was a memorial to the crew of a US Air Force Liberator bomber, killed when their aircraft crashed. Another 50 feet higher and they may have lived.

Dad also introduced me to prawning, the only outdoor activity he ever really liked. It involved the two of us going into Eastbourne at an indecently early hour, picking up a set of gin nets and two long poles, cadging some discarded plaice frames from a fishmonger and then getting ourselves to Cow Gap, the steps down to the beach from the lower grassy slopes near Beachy Head. Having baited each net with the fish bones we ventured onto the rocks, the aim being to follow the outgoing tide, placing each net - which had cork floats attached - into a rock pool. The prawns went for the fish bones; so did dozens of green crabs and other creatures including, as happened on future occasions, a large spider crab and a cuttlefish. You had to get rid of the crabs, pick out the prawns and place them in a bag, containing seaweed, which every enthusiast must have secured around their person. That was the easy part.

As I found out, the hardest part was staying upright. Wet rocks covered with wet seaweed are lethal especially if, like me on that first occasion, you were wearing rubber-soled gym shoes. I still have scars. A few years later I would become quite enthusiastic about catching prawns - the big ones could be sold to the hotels for twopence each - but that first effort yielded nothing for me and, in fact, the same for Dad. The rocks, however, provided some surprises: the formidable-looking remains of a defused mine (an anti-ship device which had broken away from its seabed anchorage) and many aluminium pieces of aircraft swept ashore from the Channel. During another trip a year later I found a near-complete gun from a Flying Fortress, complete with a 0.5-inch cartridge still in the breech.

Dad and I finally gave up on that first expedition, climbed back through Cow Gap and found somewhere to sit while we untangled the prawning gear. Another man, about Dad's age, appeared from the beach and was about 20 yards away when my father called out to him. He looked our way, frowned and asked, "Is that ….ing Goldsmith?" The man was Eddie Cole, an architect - although you wouldn't have guessed it from the way he spoke - and former companion of my father when the pair of them used to poach ducks from the lake at Hampden Park during starvation winters of the First World War. The reunion could only mean that they would be making for the nearest pub. Eddie looked at me as we rounded up the gear. "Come on, Shag," he said. I'd never been called that before. As I was to discover, he had a fund of stories - related with the use of colourful language - at which Dad and I doubled up with laughter. It really didn't matter that we had caught no prawns.

In the meantime, the Far Eastern war news was taking a strange turn with the dropping of something called an "atom bomb" on a place known as Hiroshima. It happened on Sunday, August 6th, and the newspapers had hardly finished describing how it worked and its horrific effect when the headline "Another Atom" denoted that Nagasaki had also been hit, on August 9th. In between the two events, Margaret celebrated her 8th birthday on August 8th but I cannot remember whether cake and candles were at the Hall's place or with Aunt Rose in Eastbourne.

A week later, on the 15th, it was VJ Day and despite newspaper pictures showing vast damage caused by the two new bombs there was little sympathy for the surrendering Japanese and their so-called Divine Emperor - allowed to keep his throne - who had watched his imperial forces commit atrocities wherever they landed in the Pacific. We were back in Anerley by the time Japan's formal surrender took place on board the USS Missouri on September 2nd 1945. It meant that World War 2 had lasted exactly six years, although the domestic and international echoes would rumble on for decades.

CHAPTER 21 - LIGHTING THE WAY

One of singer Vera Lynn's many wartime hit songs began, "When the lights go on again, all over the world..." It meant, of course, a much wider enlightening but there were some local authorities who couldn't wait to illuminate their streets after years of blackout. Croydon may even have made a start just before VE Day - I remember Dad taking me to the Grand Theatre there to see a production of "Hamlet" and finding that as the 654 trolleybus passed under the railway bridge near Selby Road the way ahead was lit. It wasn't exactly Blackpool seafront stuff - just a modest bulb every 100 yards or so - but it radiated optimism as well as wattage. The effect on the return journey, passing back into the gloom, was almost as depressing as the final scene in the play we had just watched.

In producing a narrative like this there are always second thoughts and bits that you feel would make it more interesting even though they don't really fit in the frame. For a start, it doesn't seem fair to leave the Thicket Road Goldsmiths stranded in September 1945 without giving some idea of what lay in store for them. Dad, for example, became involved with the Penge Urban District Council election in 1946 when three wards of six seats all became vacant at the same time. He was one of eight candidates nominated for Ward 1; there were similar numbers in the other two wards. Between the close of nominations and

Election Day, two of the other candidates in Ward 1 changed their minds and withdrew, so the remaining six - including Dad - went in unopposed. Funny, that. The other two wards had elections and Labour secured a working majority.

This majority meant that the Labour group could make decisions ahead of council meetings and nod them through regardless of anyone else's viewpoint. Dad protested against this and attacked the "sacrilegious" way in which the Vicar of Penge, the Rev I.E. Douglas-Jones, had been called in to open each meeting with prayers for heavenly guidance in decisions which had already been made. After forming the Penge and Anerley Ratepayers' Association, Dad's 17-year connection with SE20 tailed off in 1949 when he joined the Eastbourne Gazette and moved down there with Mum and Margaret.

Soon after the war, Mum's health began to suffer and it was obvious that living in a flat at the top of 15 front steps and two staircases (another 38 steps) was not good. A swap was arranged - our three-bedroom accommodation in exchange for a two-bedroom ground floor flat in Maple Road, Penge. The move was turned into a political issue by the local branch of the British Legion and, I feel, played a part in Dad's move to Eastbourne. But Mum was happy to be near members of her Arnold family, especially sister Frances.

Not long after VJ Day, Tony received his calling up papers and was sent on his way after a night out at a

London theatre - the Casino and "Starlight Roof" - courtesy of Nurse Martin, also taking Mum and Dad along. Margaret and I missed out. Despite his years in the Air Training Corps, Tony found himself in the Royal Engineers because he was - according to the tests - colour blind and not suitable for the RAF. This technical disability never harmed his work in the colour printing industry or his part-time interest in poster and water colour painting.

Uncle Jim, no longer a scruffy soldier, put in an occasional appearance while we were still living at 19 Thicket Road, as did his rather-too-sure-of-himself teenage son Lawrence. Jim's daughter Audrey and ex-wife Elsie both remained distant memories from pre-war days. In any case, Jim had acquired a new partner, Frances, plus a baby girl.

The smart-looking soldier of the family, Dan, also turned up at Thicket Road in 1947 accompanied by his Anglo-Indian wife Ethel and son Geoff, aged five or six. They had no standing in newly-independent India and their eventual arrival in London during the rush hour was a cultural shock to Ethel who had never seen so many white people in such a hurry before. "Where were they all going?" she asked. A clue to her previous lifestyle: she was equally intrigued by our gas cooker and Geoff kept referring to Mum as "Cook." The lad also declined an offer to visit our local shops, including the butcher's, because he didn't like to see animals waiting to be slaughtered. There was a lot of learning to be done.

I remember one of the less-enlightened members of the family (Shepherd's Bush branch) saying to me, "Of course, Danny married a darkie" and being surprised when I told her the facts. Ethel, bless her, was white, charming and well aware of Dan's roving eye when it came to female company. She had enough of her own money to buy and run a house in Broad Road, Lower Willingdon, and enough ability to manage The Little Shop on the nearby A22. There were quirky moments, such as her visit to a furniture shop in Eastbourne where she wanted to buy a bed-settee, known as a Put-U-Up, and asked for a sit-me-down - but I had more admiration for Ethel, and Geoff, than her eventual ex-husband.

The Halls of Hampden Park were survivors and always stuck together as a family. The eldest daughter, Peg, had married Harry, a former sailor with a wonderfully dry sense of humour. He claimed that once, on a crowded train going back to Portsmouth, he was squeezed in beside a woman trying to breastfeed a baby and that, when the child became reluctant, the mother said, "Come on! If you don't want it I'll give it to the sailor." Believe it if you like; but I was there when in a crowded back room - that back room was always crowded - the radio news bulletin announced that everything was ready for tests on Britain's first atomic bomb. Harry turned to one of the boys and remarked, "Gonna let that off at Polegate, aren't they?" Polegate, ten miles inland from Eastbourne, was the constant butt of jokes about its harbour and treacle mines.

Returning from service life and reunited with his beloved Rose and son Geoff, Uncle Tom went back to Woolworth's as manager of the Eastbourne store in Terminus Road and then a number of others before - a few years further on - he and Rose settled in Hailsham where the pair became Mayor and Mayoress.

Uncle Charlie and Aunt Vi never had children but they looked after my sister, then aged 12, when Mum was taken seriously ill. At that time Mum, Dad and Margaret were living in Eastbourne while Tony and I were living abroad and knew nothing about the crisis from which, thank heavens, Mum recovered. I once met some of Vi's family, including a brother who claimed to have been to the FA Cup Final a couple of times and watched from the grandstand without having a ticket. He went in a chauffeur's uniform and managed to mix in with all the other drivers who had taken their VIP bosses to the event and were given free seats.

In the four months between the end of the war and my starting work on December 31st 1945, Dad upped the pressure on preparing me for writing Penge and Anerley News stories. He was not a good teacher; in fact, he did not teach at all - just ripped my efforts to shreds. Having survived the school of hard knocks, he expected me to do the same, but it was not a pleasant experience. My early efforts included an interview with Roy Martin, the adopted son of Nurse Martin and recently demobilised after being a sergeant in the Queen's Regiment, serving in Italy; a piece on a singer, another ex-Army man who came to entertain our class at Oakfield with light operatic numbers; and a report on a concert by members of the Penge Pioneer Youth Club.

One of my last jobs at school was to present a specially-made gavel, block, and inkstand to the chairman of the Penge Divisional Executive of the Kent Education Committee, Alderman Frank Dixon. The whole thing had been made - very well, incidentally - by three Oakfield pupils in their woodwork centre and was to be used at the executive's Croydon Road offices. The handing-over was at an education committee meeting one Thursday evening in the council chamber at Anerley Town Hall, with the three lads attending while I had to say a few words, already written for me by Mr Margham, our headmaster. Frank Dixon thanked me for my "neat little speech" - I didn't fluff the lines - and Peter Eastment photographed the event. Soon after that it was "The Day Thou Gavest…" for the last time and Mr Margham handed me an envelope containing a reference.

It was goodbye to ten years of school and a collection of teachers, some of whom I still admire while others ranged from nondescript to certifiably peculiar. Teachers provided facts, a little guidance and occasional entertainment while - certainly at Oakfield - it was the other pupils who prepared you for life itself. I got along with most of them and had enjoyable times with classmates like Ray Sturdy, Roy D'Arcy, David Kidson, Derek Pettit, Stanley Laar and John Crayhart, plus the Thicket Road regulars.

CHAPTER 22 - THE FINAL PAGE

The first peacetime Christmas of the 1940s may have had less anxiety than those earlier in the decade, but it was still a time of austerity, ration books (they would still be around in 1954) and notices in shops which began, "Sorry, no....." Winning the war had crippled the economy and returning servicemen found that homes destroyed by bombs and rockets were not being replaced fast enough. The Labour government for which so many had voted was doing its best to bring in improvements outlined in the famous Beveridge Report but was also pursuing the idea of nationalising coal mines and railways. It had also become involved in the Tanganika Groundnut Scheme, an ill-considered plan to grow more food and oils in a part of Africa now known as Tanzania, which cost millions and produced next to nothing.

The announcement of bread rationing in 1946 was a new low. Even the Germans had failed to bring that about. Occasionally Prime Minister Clement Atlee would broadcast to the nation, but any attempt at a rallying call somehow lacked the Churchill touch. "It sounds," said Dad, "as if he is reading last week's football results."

It must have been during 1946 that Dad received a letter from Frankfurt which made us realise that even though we were short of food, conditions in Germany were bordering on the desperate. The letter was from Walter Wendel, one of the "German boys" as we called them - the other identical twin was Heinz - who had befriended Dad on his regular pre-war holidays in their country and spent a fortnight with us at Thicket Road during 1938. It was partly through them that Dad spoke and wrote such astonishingly good German. Both boys had been in the army; Heinz was killed on the Russian front and Walter was badly injured but had recovered and was married with a newly-arrived son. They lived in Mozart Strasse in Frankfurt and their little boy was called Wolfgang - naturally.

Walter meant to describe his son as a bonny baby but mis-spelled and said he was a "bony baby" - an ironic twist considering the hand-to-mouth way that all Germans were living at the time. So, what did we do - we, who had been blitzed, buzz-bombed and rocketed? We sent them a food parcel - and in his letter of thanks Walter included an extra "n" and asked it to be placed in his previous message. He and Dad did meet again during the 1950s.

Tony was still in the Army when the rest of the family moved from Thicket Road to Maple Road in 1947 or 48. It was a flat on the ground floor and had two bedrooms - one for Mum and Dad, the other for Margaret, leaving me to sleep on a cheap and very uncomfortable bed settee in the lounge. Tony was stationed at Warminster and liked to come home at weekends, having worked out a method of travelling by rail which cost only a few pence. He had by this time met Joan Quantrill, a young lady from Islington, while on holiday in Eastbourne. After a row with Dad - I wasn't there and didn't know what it was about - Tony sat in the lounge with me, had a good moan about the family's domestic arrangements and mentioned "getting hitched to Joan."

It came as quite a shock to realise that the family was breaking up. A few months later Dad's move to work in Eastbourne, where the Gazette provided a house to rent, meant his departure with Mum and Margaret on a chaotic January 1st 1949. By this time Tony, out of the Army and accommodated with longterm friends the Coopers in Evelina Road, Penge, was considering a move even further afield to a job in Cairo. I continued to work on the Penge and Anerley News, moving back to Thicket Road and staying with Mrs Shipstone and Beryl, plus the occasional visit from Dennis who had started his National Service in the RAF.

My own call-up came at the end of March, complete with a four-shilling postal order (first day's pay) and a travel warrant to Shorncliffe, near Folkestone in Kent - where Uncle Tom had joined up in 1939. I had worked hard and gained more than three years' experience as a general reporter, gradually taking on the job of covering courts, inquests, council and committee meetings, football matches (Crystal Palace in Division III South) as well as the hundred and one other matters which are the lifeblood of a local newspaper.

According to the News of the World horoscope that week, Sagittarians were due for "new opportunities, new clothes" - about the only time it had ever been right. I left the office at News Buildings in Belvedere Road,

Upper Norwood, on Friday, April 1st (don't say it) and warned my parents that I would be joining them at the seaside on Sunday, spending a few days there before meeting up on Thursday, April 7th, at Shorncliffe with a lot of anxious young men who had also received cunningly-worded invitations.

So, I was the last of the Goldsmiths to leave Thicket Road and wait in Anerley Road for the 654 trolleybus, leaving behind twelve years' worth of memories. In the years ahead, whenever I read "The House at Pooh Corner" to my children, I had to fight back the tears when it came to the final page and the leading characters departed. The Crystal Palace grounds could well be substituted for the Hundred Acre Wood but in my mind it was the stretch of Thicket Road between numbers 13A and 19 where a small boy and his friends would always be playing.

Printed in Great Britain
by Amazon

42934513R00150